D1370592

Management by Exception:
A Handbook with Forms

Management by Exception: A Handbook with Forms

DONALD P. MACKINTOSH

PRENTICE-HALL, INC. ENGLEWOOD CLIFFS, NJ

Prentice-Hall International, Inc., *London*
Prentice-Hall of Australia, Pty. Ltd., *Sydney*
Prentice-Hall of Canada, Ltd., *Toronto*
Prentice-Hall of India Private Ltd., *New Delhi*
Prentice-Hall of Japan, Inc., *Tokyo*
Whitehall Books, Ltd., *Wellington, New Zealand*
Prentice-Hall of Southeast Asia Pte. Ltd., *Singapore*

Library of Congress Cataloging in Publication Data

Mackintosh, Donald P
Management by exception.

Includes index.
1. Management by exception. I. Title.
HD38.M3143 658.4 77-25854
ISBN 0-13-548917-2

Printed in the United States of America

To Dr. T. E. Kakonis and Barbara,
my wife, whose patience and
perseverance prevailed

ABOUT THE AUTHOR

Donald P. Mackintosh is President of Brevet International, Inc., a systems design consulting firm which specializes in control management systems. He was President of Brevet Corporation & Associates, Los Angeles, before its merger with the present company.

Prior to founding Brevet Corporation & Associates in 1971, Mr. Mackintosh was Chief of Installations for the Alexander Proudfoot Company, where he acted as the firm's trouble shooter. He achieved this post in less than three years and served a total of five years in this capacity.

The author's systems experience spans two decades, in which time he has established a national reputation in innovative systems design. Among many achievements, his control system for supermarkets developed in the sixties is now used by many of the leading grocery chains in the United States, and a novel system of sustained release and production control is still being employed by firms since its inception more than a decade ago.

FOREWORD

The author of this book started a management consulting project for Thriftimart, Inc., which was to last for a year. By the end of that year many of the methods and forms contained in this book were in effect and operating in our firm. The results of the application of what is covered in this book produced a $3,000,000 savings in the first year. While the consultation fee was well over a million dollars, I feel that if I hadn't gotten a nickel savings the program would have been worth it for the training a man receives in how to run his company.

This book will expose the reader to the methods and mechanics of setting up a Management by Exception System.

Application of the forms and techniques can be used by many different industries. Use of these tools will result in good dollar return for the time and effort it takes to master them and apply them to your own operation.

In today's upward spiral of labor and material costs it is in the best interest of management to read this book, review the operation and apply the rules and mechanics spelled out in *Management by Exception: A Handbook with Forms*. It will be time profitably spent.

Robert E. Laverty

Chairman of the Board
Thriftimart, Inc.

WHAT THIS BOOK WILL DO FOR YOU

This book gives you the step by step method of setting up and using a system of Management by Exception. It has been written with the objective of smoother operation, lower costs and higher profits being available to the user. All levels of management and systems managers will benefit from the use of this handbook with forms.

The large corporation president down to the head of the smallest department can follow through the development of an exception system in his own operation. If improvement is the motive, the manager has his guidelines set up. He can add the knowledge of his own operation to the material written into this book and move forward into higher profits and a smoother, more productive operation.

How can you follow the book to layout your own system? What methods are available? What will it do for you? A few answers to these questions are given in the following checklist.

The book spells out the ground rules for Management by Exception. This is done through definition of the objective, which is to manage by exception. A firm rule is spelled out: *A plan must be in place*. The failure to acknowledge and apply this rule is highlighted. See Chapter 1.

The book alerts you to the comparison of the work load with the work hours. This comparison is an initial step to establishing a plan. See Figure 1.

The book shows how to look at input variances before establishing a plan. See Figure 2.

A simple hourly plan is spelled out which involves the employees and sets hourly goals. See Figure 3.

The book points out what to do when the work runs out before the day is over. See Chapter 1.

It further shows examples of false exception systems and how to identify them. See Chapter 1.

Exception reports in place with no plan behind them are identified so you can use those in existence to build a plan. See Chapter 1.

The book explains how to marry the chain of command to the detail of the plan. See Figure 4.

A method of establishing the true time of an operation is explained in the book. See Chapter 2.

Diagram A reflects how simply an interdepartment planning system can be detailed.

The book spells out what happens to plans that have not been detailed to a point of execution. See Chapter 2.

Figure 5 shows how plotting hourly outputs can pre-identify where hidden exceptions lie.

The book reveals why you must revise your plans as time and circumstance change the conditions. See Chapter 2.

The book sets up some quick rules to be applied to all reporting. See Chapter 2.

Figure 7 shows how to breathe life into your annual budget.

The book tells how to collect seemingly unrelated information to obtain hidden causes of profit loss. See Chapter 2.

The steps of implementing an exception system are spelled out in Chapter 2.

The book spells out several methods of categorizing exceptions to produce a picture requiring attention. See Figures 9 and 10.

The book develops the results of allowing exception actions to continue without documentation. See Chapter 3.

How to certify facts on reports for cost improvement is explained in Chapter 3.

Figure 11 spells out a simple method of reducing your copier costs.

Simple rules are spelled out when documenting your system in Chapter 3.

The book tells how to pre-determine exceptions so reporting can be concise. See Chapter 4.

Furthermore, Chapter 4 tells how to anticipate exceptions as well as pre-determine them.

How to take all the exceptions and group them into ten categories is explained in Chapter 4.

The book tells how to categorize salesmen's problems through the use of a cause code. See Figure 13.

How to identify and solve your firm's largest problem is covered in Chapter 5.

The book tells how to force major problems to the surface. See Chapter 5.

How to identify the major company problems in a multiple location operation is covered in Chapter 5, Figure 15.

The book points out how to establish cross checks on exception reporting. See Chapter 6.

How to identify human element in an exception system is covered in Chapter 6.

The book deals with the methods of involving all levels of management in an exception system in Chapter 6.

How to analyze work loads and determine self generated peaks and valleys is illustrated in Figures 16 and 17.

The book illustrates how to use effective employee tallies in Figures 18 and 19.

The book details how to capture and use customer volume information to set up an exception system through the use of Figures 20 and 21.

A curving guide is shown which reflects the use in planning to give good customer service in Figure 22.

How to use standard data information is shown in Figure 23 and covered in Chapter 6.

The book shows how to plot sales goals and personnel requirements which will trigger adding or subtracting from the work force to achieve the volume at the anticipated costs. See Chapter 7.

How to determine the impact on other departments when sales are made is illustrated in Figure 25.

The book shows a method of determining the cause of uneven work loads and reflects the solution, once the cause is identified in Figures 26 and 27.

How problems in one department can identify the real cause of low productivity in another department is covered in Chapter 7.

Further, Figure 28 shows how exceptions will direct management from one area to another.

How to plan specifics in order to verify your rules of thumb is shown in Chapter 8, Figures 30, 31, 32 and 33.

The book shows how time related schedules will identify exceptions in Chapter 8, Figures 34 and 35.

How to break a construction estimate down to the point of controllable execution is covered in Chapter 8.

The book spells out how to use the computer to break down and follow the detail in Chapter 8.

The book shows a method of identifying weak supervision through comparison. See Chapter 8, Figure 39.

How to establish the relationships between disciplines as a method of exception audit is covered in Chapter 9, Figures 40 and 41.

The book covers how to use sets of operating figures to set up a Management by Exception System in accounting. See Chapter 9, Figures 42, 43 and 45.

How to look at the total picture on a single sheet of paper is shown in Figure 46.

The book deals with the dancing dollar and how to make it stand still for evaluation purposes in Chapter 9.

Figure 48 covers the real cost of fringe benefits and how to determine them.

The book ends with the annual report and how to apply a Management by Exception System to one. See Chapter 9, Figures 49 and 50.

Each chapter takes you deeper into the world of Management by Exception. The mechanics and forms used to solve the problems are easy to follow, and lead you from initial identification of the basics to the full use and application of the system. Each example and form can be readily adapted to the reader's use for implementation into his own operation.

HOW THIS BOOK IS ORGANIZED

Management by Exception: A Handbook with Forms is organized into nine chapters. Each chapter leads further into the use and application of a total Management by Exception System. In each chapter rules are laid down, examples spelled out and case histories examined. Charts, diagrams and forms are added so the reader may start from the first chapter to apply the system to his own area. The forms are laid out so only the headings have to be changes in order to be used. Each form in the book has been tested under fire and proven to be successful in its application. As the reader progresses through the book, a chapter summary is included as a memory jogger. Each chapter builds on the former. It is recommended that the book be read through first and then be taken as a check sheet through the reader's operation.

For example, take Chapter 1. This is entitled Management by Exception: Establishing the Ground Rules. It begins with a definition of the desired end result of a system. From this point, development through examples and cases of the necessity of establishing a plan is firmly laid down. The results of failure to do so are also shown. A diagram reflecting time and work load, a graph showing volume variance and a simple plan to actual form are covered. The basics are now introduced. As the other chapters unfold, the forms and their implementation will grow more complex, but not more difficult. In this first chapter, the reader is introduced into the field of Management by Exception and will have an opportunity to copy the first three illustrations, and put them to use in his own operation.

Or look at Chapter 9, Management by Exception in the Financial Aspects of the Business, where the former chapters have laid out methods and provided forms for the reader. Now the use of the system lends itself to the management of the life blood of the company. Here the use of the fluctuating dollars or fringe benefits plays a part. This chapter contains an illustration of a form in which the sales, administration, manufacturing, cash flow and all the exceptions of a company's many facets are brought together on a single top management report.

Woven through all chapters is the dollar value of application of a Management by Exception System. Each of the chapters covers a further step into a total Management by Exception System, each chapter with new illustrations and usable forms. Here is a book organized for use either in whole or in part. The value of using more of the tools will become clear as the dollar improvement in your operation increases.

HOW TO USE THIS BOOK

The preceding pages told you what this book will do for you and how this book is organized. Now consider the following possible uses of the book. . .

1. If you have a specific problem, for example, "How can you cut down check stand lines without increasing your payroll?", turn to the check list of forms or the index, and look for the appropriate form. In this case, the customer dollar recap in Chapter 6 would apply. Turn to Chapter 6 and read the mechanics of the why and how to use the form. Then, review your own check stand problems. The use of a flow format, as illustrated in Diagram A of Chapter 2, would be helpful. Once you have made this comparison, you are ready to implement the changes outlined in the book. Similar questions can be followed through in the same manner throughout the book.
2. If your operation is starting to bog down, the profits are seeping away, you should read through the entire book. As you read the book, make margin notes when you encounter problems similar to yours. Where you note a problem which may be in your operation, but you are not sure, use the methods of identification spelled out in the book to check your own area. Once this read through has been accomplished, select the major problem you have identified as the first area to change. Using the rules spelled out, adapt the headings of the forms to your own operation. Have

all the supervisory personnel involved read the pages in the book pertaining to the problem. After this has been done, implement the form and follow through on the mechanics.

3. If your problem is one where your managers are not showing improvement in their operations, set up a nine week class using the book as the text. Select one individual to hold the sessions each week. Distribute copies of the book to all who are joining in this program of training. Cover one chapter of the book each week. Have each person comment on each chapter as it relates to their area or department.
4. If you are receiving a myriad of reports, and none of them seem to be doing the job, use the book to audit the rules of reporting spelled out. When you have critically evaluated the reports you are receiving against these rules, determine why the current reports are lacking. You will then be able to look over a dozen reporting formats in the book to compare how to modify your current reports, or use one or more of those illustrated in the book. If you use only one of the 50 forms or diagrams in this book, it will be well worth the price of the book. These forms and diagrams are for your use, and when used, will repay you for your efforts many times.

Dramatic dollar return will be your reward for implementing the systematic practices and procedures that make up Management by Exception. More efficient, more productive operation is the name of the game—this handbook contains the answers that will help you reach this worthy objective.

Donald P. Mackintosh

CONTENTS

TABLE OF FIGURES

Management by Exception:
A Handbook with Forms

1

MANAGEMENT BY EXCEPTION: ESTABLISHING THE GROUND RULES

WHY THIS BOOK IS WRITTEN

This handbook has been written to help focus the professional manager and the systems man on the basic methods of establishing a Management by Exception System. Some of the forms and examples should highlight situations in his own operation. Hopefully, it will point the way to solutions as well. It is understood that the area of undertaking may appear complex. No matter how complex or difficult one must never lose sight of the simple rule of a Management by Exception System: In the absence of a plan, there can be no exceptions.

DEFINITION

Management by Exception is a method of using exceptions to control the operation. It can be the culmination of an operating system, where interruptions to the completion of a plan are identified at the point of initial execution. These interruptions or exceptions can be collected and carried forward to all levels of management. If properly identified and grouped, these exceptions can be either eliminated or must be included in future plans. Management by Exception is the method of making management face the impact of problems.

TO MANAGE BY EXCEPTION THE RULE OR PLAN MUST BE IN PLACE

Exceptions cannot exist without rules or, in the language of business, plans. Those plans must first be clearly understood by and communicated to all personnel who will work intimately with them, and so, while this handbook deals with management by exception, we must begin with the establishment of a plan from which exceptions will inevitably occur. If you will consider for a moment some of the routine activities in your daily life, you will be struck by just how well you yourself are already managing by exception, primarily because you work from an initial plan. Most people, for example, manage to get to work on time, and their ability to accomplish this routine yet vital act, indicates the existence of a plan taken successfully to execution. On the rare occasions one is late, an exception to that plan has occurred: the alarm fails to go off (though just possibly it wasn't set) or the weather is bad (though last night's weather report may have been ignored) or the traffic jammed (though the holiday weekend was overlooked). Doubtless, you can conceive of many more exceptions to the plan to be at work on time, but the point is the individual offering such exceptions/excuses doesn't understand that, once the plan is set in motion, its maintenance consists of exercising those exceptions for the ultimate purpose of keeping the plan functioning properly.

MANAGEMENT BY EXCEPTION CANNOT OCCUR WITHOUT A PLAN: SOME FAMILIAR EXAMPLES

To accept as valid the excuses offered by the tardy employee would be to turn one's back on the whole concept of Management by Exception. First, there is the possibility that some employees (and we shall see later, some full business operations) are attempting to function without the plan at all. The simplest means of detecting this flaw is to note the almost continuous recurrence of the exceptions themselves. In the case of the tardy employee, some brief, pointed questioning by the supervisor will usually reveal the absence of a plan and, assuming the employee desires to keep his job, corrective action ordinarily takes the form of simply establishing a plan in the employee's mind. Not long ago a Chicago firm set up a West Coast division and ran an ad in the Los Angeles *Times* for prospective employees. Interviews were arranged and the firm's managers were appalled by the consistent tardiness of the would-be employees. Still, it was necessary to staff the division and some of the late arrivals were hired. Three years later the division was closed as unprofitable. Not surprising, those late arrivals for the interviews carried their habits of poor planning over into the operations of the firm, and a very unfavorable performance for the division resulted. Those employees had apparently never learned to establish a plan and to manage it by exception.

AN EXAMPLE CLOSE TO HOME

Another example that should be familiar to most readers concerns the distribution of household expense money. Oftentimes, a detailed documentation of all the money spent is paraded about as proof of a plan. One is tempted to wonder how many marital squabbles are settled—however temporarily—by that oft-quoted phrase: "I can tell you where every penny of that money went. . . ." Such a notion may soothe a bristling spouse for a time, but it is a sad truth that the detailing of expenses is no substitute for a plan. If there is to be any exercising of judgment as to where and how money should be spent, a plan is as necessary at the household level as at the business level. If that plan is built around expenses that may reasonably be expected, then family collisions over, for example, guitar lessons can be avoided. The lessons may be construed as an exception to the plan for entertainment, and hopefully, rational judgment will be applied regarding availability of funds for that purpose.

FAILURE TO OPERATE WITH ADVANCE PLAN IN BUSINESS

One can extend this domestic example to businesses in general. Many companies employ a battery of bookkeepers whose function is to account for the various expenditures incurred in the business operation, and yet top management people often haven't the foggiest conception of what precisely their products cost. In point of fact, many managers, when asked that question by irate stockholders, will answer after the fashion of the embattled housewife: "I can account for every penny of the money we have spent." If the line sounds familiar, the results are also much the same, though somehow in business those simple, revealing words impress many with their "profundity," perhaps because the same ideas are couched in different language: "Our last operating statement reflects a slight upturn in the cost of automobile production caused by new labor agreements and a rise in steel prices, which necessitates an obvious increase of 3.2% in the price of this year's Road Streakers or an average increase of $138.15 per model. . . ." Sure enough, there it is—"I can account for every penny of it. . . ." But where was the advance plan in either the kitchen or the Road Streaker factory?

DRAMATIC TURNAROUND VIA MANAGEMENT BY EXCEPTION

A small Midwestern injection mold plastics company was caught in a habitual late delivery pattern. In despair, the management called in a group of systems people to determine why, regardless of demand, almost all orders were shipped late. Through a brief tour of the plant and an interview with all levels of management and the employees on the machines, it was quickly determined that no one in the chain of command from the president to the machine operator had the remotest conception of what should be produced, except by category of what was assigned to the machine. The president knew that the McCulloch saw handle part had to be shipped by next Thursday. The plant manager knew that this same part was assigned to machine #3 for three shifts. The foreman of the shift during the interview knew who was assigned to this machine. The machine operator knew what problems were existing in today's production, but no one from top to bottom knew any of the material aspects of the plan. A) The president didn't know when the product could be produced. B) The plant manager didn't know how many pieces should have been produced in the last work day. C) The foreman didn't know how many he was to produce during this shift. D) The employee didn't know how many they had produced at all, let alone how many they should have produced. Here was a typical example of what is occurring today in American business. Desires, hopes, necessities and commitments are being substituted for plans. Needless to say, this plant's reputation had been built on the absence of any type of plan whatsoever, and its market position was rapidly deteriorating because of its inability to keep its commitments or produce and ship on schedule.

Once a plan had been put in place, this plant experienced a dramatic turnaround. Production schedules were set and met. At the machine operator level, the piece count was set for each hour. In a very short time, heretofore unknown exceptions were being handled, and the profits of this plant doubled in the following twelve months.

Aside from the profit increase, this plant gained a reputation as an on time delivery plant. Employee participation grew into enthusiasm, which reflected itself in substantial piece count improvement each hour.

Perhaps the largest number of people employed in a single endeavor in the United States, where there is a total absence of planning, are those people commonly referred to as outside salesmen. The situation, although employing different terms, remains basically the same. The president knows what has to be sold to keep his company operating at profit. The sales manager having gone through a detailed budgetary procedure usually knows the volume required by quarter or month from his sales force. This generally is divided by the number of salesmen, somewhat altered by impressions, knowledge and history of individual sales territories and assigned to the individual salesman. While apparently operating under a planning system, in essence, it is nothing more than an exercise in long division. From the president to the newest hired salesman, there is a total absence of a functional plan. Goals, desires and needs have been substituted for basic management predictions of what is to be accomplished. All the sales meetings, pep rallies and incentive systems used today to motivate and direct sales forces are a total waste of money in the absence of a single operating plan, which breaks down the requirements to a point of sales execution in front of a buying customer. The only exception reporting possible with this method of sales planning is the inevitable type apologizing—"Our sales did not meet anticipated levels this past quarter''—from the salesman to the sales manager to the president to the shareholders.

CUSTOMER COMPLAINTS UNDERSCORE ABSENCE OF A PLAN

The absence of a plan is most easily identified at the consumer level. Late deliveries or repeated irregular deliveries from vendors or merchants invariably are clear indications of the absence of an operating plan, which, while it can have late shipments, would certainly not repeat them. Further evidence of the absence of planning can be quickly verified through a telephone call to the sending company requesting information as to when the product ordered will arrive. The more vague the answers, the more indelibly an identification has been made of an absence of an operating plan in place, which would predict the shipment or arrival date of the desired item. ''We are checking on that now . . . Let me get back to . . . When did you order that . . . I can't understand that, that was entered into production on the 3rd. . . .'' These all too familiar phrases are clear indications that not only is there not a Management by Exception mechanism in place which would eliminate this from happening again, but there isn't even a plan in operation which might have eliminated it in the first place.

WHAT WILL CONTROL OF THE EXCEPTION ACCOMPLISH?

The reasons for putting a plan in place are two-fold. The first insures the best thinking of those initially responsible, and the second highlights exceptions as they occur, and as they are later fed back into a revision of the original plan. This book is primarily concerned with the use and control of exceptions, and, therefore, no detailed explanation of planning tools will be attempted here; however, the forms, which will subsequently be explained, assume a plan in place. Control of any exception improves the plan, and such control places the efforts of the planner and, hence, of the entire operation in better, more productive perspective. Later chapters will demonstrate how this approach may be applied to service operations, manufacturing, sales, financing and almost every other aspect of business, even if an aspect is particular and unique and will never occur again. Control of exceptions will put the planner in a position to realize when he is going off schedule and to set off an alarm system for new thinking *before* costs get out of hand. Another way to look at exception controls is to compare them with the signal arm and lights at a railroad crossing. All that flashing and clamor are there to signal the motorist that an exception to his plan to cross the tracks has occurred. Once a plan is in place, the railroad crossing signs have, in effect, been established; when an exception occurs, the bells and the lights dramatically indicate a warning. If one is to manage successfully by exception, those signs must be built into the plan.

A BEFORE AND AFTER CASE

A. The problem

A major grocery chain operating in the southern California market had a centralized paper baling operation located near their produce and meat distribution center. The company followed the practice of tearing cardboard boxes flat in the several stores, placing the cardboard in huge canvas slings and returning the paper on the empty produce delivery trucks. These slings were dumped on the ground at the baler and later scooped into a forty-foot pit, where they were crushed into thousand pound bales. Before initiating a system of Management Control by Exception, this operation had gotten so out of hand that a veritable mountain of unbaled paper towered over the warehousing complex. When the personnel in charge were asked why such a situation was allowed to exist, they replied that it was an example of the work fitting the time and that, in theory, there was no solution short of hiring more labor to clean up the mess. Clearly, this approach was getting them nowhere, and the growing mountain of paper was mute testimony to its failure. Ultimately, complaints were filed against the company, for the wet, soggy, unbaled paper became a breeding ground for rats. The president chose to apply his Management by Exception training to the problem of the baler and assigned his systems manager the task of cleaning up the mess and seeing to it that it did not reoccur.

B. The solution

All phases of the operation were included in the solution, from the accounting to the shipping of the baled paper. It was first discovered that no plan, formal or otherwise, existed other than the blind notion that whatever paper was returned from some fifty stores was to be eventually baled. The employees arrived at the baling center at 6 a.m. and worked until 3 p.m., with an hour off for lunch; anything after three was overtime. A simple plan revealed the usual arrival times of the returning trucks. The earliest truck returned to the baler at 1 p.m. and the latest was in by 5 p.m. This, then, was the first major exception noted in making a plan (see Figure 1), for the fact was, that no matter how efficiently the employees worked, they had only two hours (from 1 to 3 p.m.) during which the work was available, and they were on regular time. The discovery of this exception solved the riddle of the growing pile of paper; the next step was to determine what amount of input arrived on a day-to-day basis. This determination reflected an irregular input pattern (see Figure 2), which meant, that even if the work hours were matched to the work input, on Monday there would be ninety bags to bale, while on Wednesday there would be only about forty, or less than half the

Offset Time Table

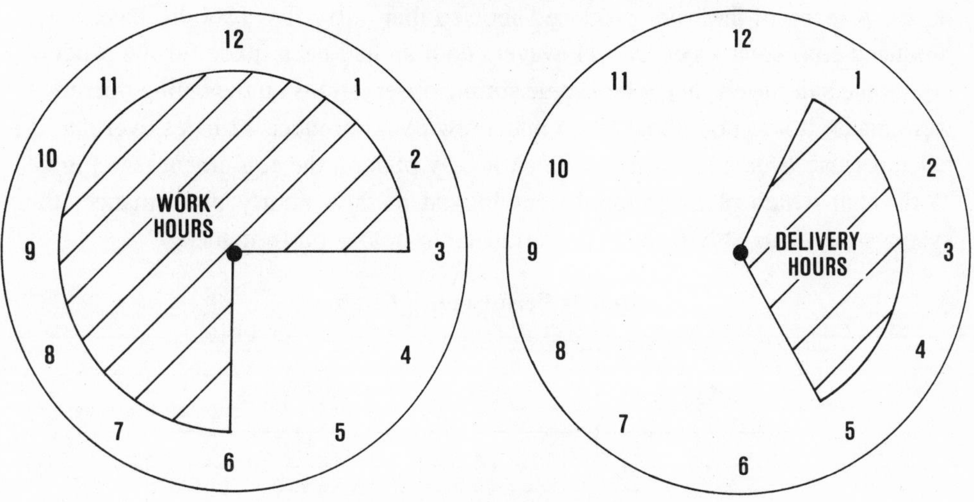

FIGURE 1

Day-To-Day Variance Graph

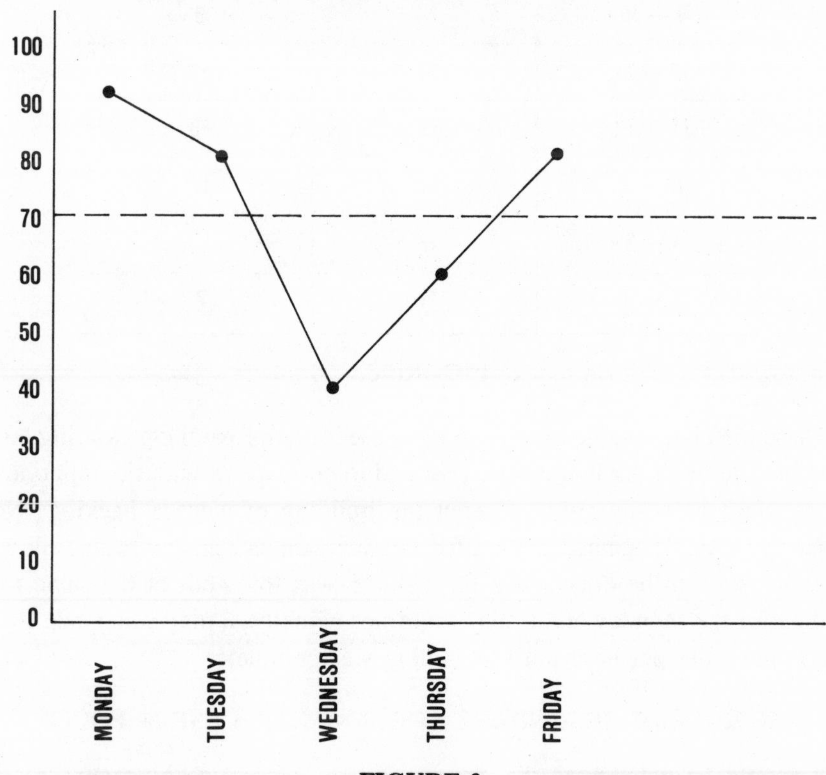

FIGURE 2

Monday figure. Here was yet another reason for the burgeoning mountain of paper. A recap of the bales produced showed that thirty-five 1000 lb. bales were produced consistently per day. However, no plan had been made for the production of the baler itself, and when some simple observations on the baling operation were made, it was noted that a two man crew could produce 12 bales over the 35 bales per day average. By imposing an hourly plan on the equipment (see Figure 3) through which plan the employees logged in their hourly performance, the systems man was able to identify variances in hourly performance.

Hourly Performance Chart

TIME	PLAN	ACTUAL
6 — 7	12	10
7 — 8	12	12
8 — 9	12	8
9 — 10	12	6
10 — 11	12	12
11 — 12	12	10
12 — 1	12	12
1 — 2	12	7
2 — 3	12	8

FIGURE 3

These then became the exception tools used to improve the prevailing conditions. First, the working hours were changed to correspond with the input hours, allowing work to be available without the building of a large backlog. Next, Wednesdays were designated as days for area maintenance and paint-up, allowing the routine work to be done when the volume was low and, at the same time, providing for the Monday and Friday build-ups. Finally, a plan was made for the baling of ten bales per hour until the baling was complete.

THE ROLE OF SECONDARY ASSIGNMENTS: CASE IN POINT

It should be noted here that a common mistake made by managers is to decrease the amount required per hour, on the assumption that the work will run out. In this case secondary assignments were provided, and the baling rate was maintained until all the paper was gone, at which time a new, nonbaling assignment was waiting. With this new method of managing the area by exception, the former crewing was too large. The operation had taken the equivalent of 180 hours of regular pay per week at a rate of $3 per hour, which meant that each bale had a labor cost of approximately $3 per bale. Once the backlog was cleaned up and details of the operation worked out and managed by exception, the total hours were reduced to 80 straight time hours per week for the same baling rate. Costs, therefore, were reduced to a little under $1.40 per bale for a saving of about $1.71 per bale or $299.25 per week or $15,561 per year. Such dramatic savings were achieved through the application of the rules of Management Control by Exception on the part of a systems man, and they were achieved in the span of less than two weeks—no small return on the employer's investment.

CASE STUDY OF A COMPANY THAT ATTEMPTED MANAGEMENT BY EXCEPTION BEFORE THE PLAN WAS IN PLACE

A large plastic and rubber gasket fitting manufacturer had outgrown its production plant. While they had a relatively good system of Managing by Exception, that system had slipped down to the foreman level to the extent that top management was no longer directly involved. The original system had been designed and implemented by an outside firm some years before, and the company's own systems men were not consulted in planning the move. From their location in the old manufacturing area of the city, the company was going to relocate in a new industrial park in a suburb some 40 miles to the east. In order to accomplish this move, an engineering firm had been employed to work out the details. That firm had a national reputation, yet they interpreted their assignment as a relocation of the equipment and physical plant only. No consideration whatsoever was given to the necessity of establishing a detailed plan to include everything necessary for getting back into production. When queried about the lack of such a plan, the president of this operation replied that he had hired the engineering firm, and they were on a guarantee basis. All the same, the engineering firm never had to pay a dime on the guarantee, but the plant in question almost went bankrupt before it was able to make deliveries again.

THE NECESSITY FOR AN OVERALL PLAN

What was the cause of this near disaster? The reason was so simple and obvious it had been overlooked by the top management. No overall plan existed, merely a single one for the equipment move itself. When the raw material was not available, or the power was not turned on, or the new personnel not trained, or the packing boxes missing, or any of the multitude of other production details unattended to, no one knew what to do or whom to call. Yet the equipment *was* in place. The top management had told all its personnel to call either the engineers or themselves personally if any problems arose. They assured their people they would manage the move by exception! Exception to what? Shortly after the move was effected, the president was phoned by the individual who had urged the necessity of detailing a move. The president was out of breath, excited and clearly quite upset. "I haven't had a minute to do anything since we moved," he said, "I've been down here on the production floor trying to get out some of our gaskets before we lose any more of our customers." How much less effort and grief he would have had, if he had detailed a plan and then operated it by exception, rather than attempting to rely on the machine move by an outside firm. He hadn't heard of any major exceptions on the move, but this was only natural since he had not worked out anything but the equipment move. There were no alarm bells going off at the right time to notify him that the plan—had there been one—was going wrong. Without a plan, there can be no Management Control by Exception; a detailed plan of a single element will simply not suffice as a substitute for the whole.

COMMON ATTEMPTS TO USE MANAGEMENT BY EXCEPTION

A systems man analyzing his own operation will almost certainly come across several exception reporting mechanisms. Some examples of these are seen in the various disciplines at work within a typical operation. Consider the Personnel Department. Here you find such exception devices as Accident Reports, Lost Time Reports, Sick Day Reports and Sick Leave Reports, all evidence of an attempt to use exception reporting, however, unconsciously. In that same department you may also find the absence of an overall plan for the crewing of the entire operation or a particular sub-department. As a matter of fact, don't be too surprised to find that no one knows for certain what the current population of the company is, simply because there is no plan calling for that information in the first place. If you feel the personnel manager has been remiss in his duties, consider next the accounting department. Here too, you will likely find ample evidence of exception reporting: Aged Receivables Reports, Bad Check Reports, Manufacturing Variances, Audit Irregularities. All of these reports and devices are vital to any operation, vital in the same way the engineering firm's move of the manufacturing equipment was important to the gasket company's relocation move. But unless they are tied to an overall plan that includes all of these exception techniques, they will only do a partial job.

In almost every industry, one will find attempts to use Management by Exception. Many such attempts appear to be valid, but one must remember that if they are in fact a real part of managing by exception, the plan must first be in place. A Sick Days Report, that only tallies how many sick days are being taken, is of no help to the manager who wishes to plan for so many days of sick time in his operation, and who is prepared to take action when that sick time exceeds his plan. In reading the endless "Aged Receivable Reports" in business today, it becomes painfully clear that far too many managements have never established a plan for what the amount of aged receivables should be. Rather, their reaction is to recoil in horror at what it is, at a time when it is too late to exercise any constructive management decisions to alleviate the situation. Now, all they can do is direct their efforts to cleaning up the past due account.

TWO CASES IN POINT

The whole system of credit bureaus and their notable extensions, such as Dun and Bradstreet, is evidence of the failure of most managements to have a plan for past due accounts. If the time, money and effort spent to collect bad debts and overdue accounts were expended in making a firm plan and taking action at the first early warning signs, much less loss would be experienced. One manager of a West Coast region of a major telephone company stated, off the record, that 10% of the total revenues billed in his area were never collected. With a knowing smile he added, "You know who has to pay for that loss, don't you? The people who pay their bills." Telephone companies pride themselves on the fact that they can pinpoint a problem by noting the exceptions. In theory, at least, a malfunctioning telephone, if reported, will have a pattern built in time which will pinpoint where the problem originates and why. One can get a detailed explanation of this superb system by simply calling an operator, complaining of a malfunctioning telephone and asking to speak to the supervisor. Unfortunately, however, the telephone companies do not have the complete system of Management by Exception in place, and the malfunctions continue as do the elaborate lectures of the supervisors. Those lectures sound so convincing they often become believable—until the next inevitable malfunction. After a hearing on a rate increase for one telephone company, a judge ruled that this would be the last increase until the company's service gave evidence that an attempt was being made to serve the public, rather than disregard its complaints. Evidently, the judge hadn't had an explanation by the supervisor regarding the exception system employed to solve the company's numerous complaints.

The national credit companies provide another example of an illstarred attempt to manage by exception. They are particularly exemplary of the accounting field, in which Management by Exception can run completely out of control until the operation takes on a nightmarish aspect. A large credit card company once had a late payment reminder cross lines in the mail between their credit collection people in Florida and their billing operation in Arizona. The payment for a month's bill was mailed two days prior to the new statements coming out. The exception reporting system notified the proper agencies to send out a "your bill is overdue" statement, which was repeated monthly for three months. By the end of the third month, the card holder, who had paid his bill each month, was in possession of some harshly worded cards and letters from Florida, each with the preemptory order to return the card. Once the fury of this system was unleased, no amount of explanatory letters was adequate to quell it. This is a classic example of the exception system gone wild and, sad to say, is not an isolated case. Other examples of computer billing mercilessly attacking an individual due to an exception in the billing process are familiar to anyone who reads the newspapers.

MISCONCEPTIONS ABOUT MANAGEMENT BY EXCEPTION

The first misconception normally encountered in Management by Exception systems is the blind belief that an exception can of itself serve to initiate an action. This false view can be traced invariably to the absence of an original plan. It must be understood that an exception exists because of the failure of a plan or the lack of one. In the examples of the telephone companies and credit card accounting systems cited above, there was no plan which would prevent those uncollected amounts from becoming so large in the first place. The instantaneous reaction of the credit companies, on the other hand, suggests the absence of a plan for review. In both cases, there appears to be a need for the use of a simple credit report: for the telephone company to prevent the loss before it occurred, and for the credit card company, as a review, to determine if the expected card holder is a bad debt or if there is an error in the system.

CASE IN POINT

There are those who feel it is possible to manage by exception without a plan. One major consulting firm headquartered in Chicago was fined by the government for working its new staff personnel long hours without paying them overtime. Since this firm had no basic operating policies and no formal company plan, it was forced to have all its managers submit a detailed accounting for the staff time thereafter. The firm mistakenly believed that this was operating by exception; it never occurred to them that the submissions of a plan would have placed them in a far stronger position. The manager's reports could then have detailed any exceptions. Need it be added, they received their second fine two years later for the identical reason? All their detailed reporting had gone for nothing, for they had no plan to back up after-the-fact reporting which was touted as Management by Exception. When it passed the federal reviewing stand, it failed to get the salute.

THE COMPUTER AS VILLAIN

In the first and second generation of the computer industry, a proliferation of paper descended upon management with an endless deluge of facts regarding its operations. Managers had to wade through countless sheets of IBM size paper to get to an essential bit of information, and many companies threw out the entire data processing system because of its production of masses of useless and confusing detail. This situation was an unfortunate example of reported totals, obscuring the fact that no plan was in place to reflect only the exceptions. Sales reporting systems are particularly prone to this type of weakness. A computerized sales reporting system can become a nightmare of facts, calls, sales, geography, clients, auto usage, air fare, back orders and whatever else is deemed necessary to know in order to run a sales force. And all too often, when elaborate systems of this sort are found, a plan is absent.

CASE IN POINT

A space heater company located in the Midwest had a national sales force working the backwoods of the country. The company's sales had been going well, and it was felt that an investment in a data processing reporting system would help increase sales even more. They installed the second generation system which employed tub files of key punched cards, and this system produced reports better weighed than read. After a year of all this, the company lost sales for the first time in history. The management discovered that while they were looking at all the facts, they had neglected to consider the exceptions. In the past they had kept a simple tally at the order desk, which told everyone concerned who was selling and where. From that original system they had been able to pinpoint an exception, involve management and get the problem corrected. Under the new data processing method, they were told so much more than merely the naked sales figures, they stopped looking at the sales, abandoned exceptions, learned far too much of the details of each and every area and lost sight of the only reason for the sales force in the first place—*Sales*. They had become so involved with totals they no longer saw the exceptions. Ultimately, the president threw out the computer, tub files and, with them, the sales manager; and now, with a modified though essentially similar version of their original plan, they have increased sales once again.

While the computer made it easier for management to lose sight of the plan and its exceptions, the computer itself is nothing more than an available tool and is not, in fact, the villain. In many companies the top manager possesses all the operating facts of his areas and yet never sees where he can improve or where his talents are needed. When such is the case, one can be certain that this manager is in possession of too many of the day-to-day facts of the operation and not in control of the overall plan. Remember the personnel department manager who has all those reports and still knows nothing of the total population of the company?

He is simply another example of knowing all about the total detail and nothing about the exceptions which direct one to the problem.

COCKTAIL PARTY TALK

At a recent meeting of hospital administrators, a systems man was discussing the use of exception reporting informally with some of the people present. Overhearing the talk, one of the administrators remarked wisely, "You know, of course, that there are several schools of thought on exception reporting." The systems man took this statement as a challenge. Through a series of deft, pointed questions he discovered that the administrator was all but ignorant of the several "schools of thought" he had referred to so cavalierly and of the fundamental elements of exception reporting as well. All too often, one hears glib talk about managing an operation by exception, and such talk gives rise to the impression that nothing could be easier to implement and to profit from than a management control system of exception. Quite the contrary. A good deal of planning and tuning are required to make an exception system work. In the following chapters we will consider some of the techniques to be applied in implementing such a system.

MANAGEMENT BY EXCEPTION POINTERS

1. Exceptions cannot exist without plans.
2. The plan must be fully established and understood by all concerned *before* exception reporting begins.
3. Detailed planning insures the best thinking of those responsible and highlights exceptions as they occur. Such exceptions can then contribute to a revision of the original plan.
4. The establishment of reasonable secondary assignments can reduce the work force and consequently labor costs.
5. There is no substitute for an overall plan. Partial planning can result in disastrous losses in production.
6. Exception reporting techniques are often employed without an understanding of their role in the overall plan. To be effective, they must be used in conjunction with that plan.
7. Exceptions cannot, of themselves, serve to initiate action.
8. Masses of detailed facts and information are not necessarily helpful in pinpointing exceptions. Only such information pertinent to the workings of the overall plan is required for the discovery of exceptions.

2

SETTING UP AND MONITORING A SYSTEM OF MANAGEMENT BY EXCEPTION

ESTABLISHING THE PLAN

Establish the plan—this is the first and most important rule in any system of Management Control by Exception. Consider once more the simple example of getting to work on time. No matter how simple this daily procedure may seem, it would be all but impossible without a plan. In this case, the plan is of the most informal nature and is almost never committed to writing or reviewed with anyone else. Yet the elements of a plan are still there and in place. There is, for example, historical knowledge. Certainly, driving to work in the morning requires some knowledge of what transpired on the chosen route in the past. Then, there are the site conditions, such as the state of the road along the way, the weather for the day, traffic patterns, stop lights and so on. In addition to these, equipment knowledge is vital, for a poorly functioning vehicle is a factor which must surely be taken into account. Both site conditions and equipment fall into the broader classification of field knowledge, thus one is left with the two bigger elements of historical information and field knowledge. No matter how simple or how complex the establishment of a plan may be, these two elements must always be present and consulted in order to construct a plan.

THE USES OF HISTORICAL INFORMATION AND FIELD KNOWLEDGE

In very complex planning procedures whole departments are engaged in either detailing the history of the plan or setting up site conditions, thus bringing the field knowledge into play. A small manufacturing operation may have the plant manager draw upon his systems personnel as well as his production control department before he releases his next week's production schedule. Over the years the direct relationship between the management of a plant and such supporting areas may have become remote, but they are, nevertheless, all extensions of the plant manager's production plan. Certainly, there are numerous instances in which the plant manager looks upon the systems people or the production control department as something other than an extension of his planning.

CASE IN POINT

In a large hardware fitting manufacturing operation, production control was releasing orders independently of the plant management. Some systems people were called in to help reduce the massive in process volume. Their task was nothing more than convincing the plant manager to make the overall plan and to allow the production control department to detail it, rather that create it independently. The results in this particular plant were extremely gratifying, as the reduction of work in process amounted to well over $250,000.

BREAKING THE CHAIN OF COMMAND

One basic deterrent to the establishment of a plan is the crossing of the chain of command at various levels. In the example of the hardware fitting operation, the production control department was not subordinate to the plant manager, but was rather acting independently in the releasing of orders. One can see that the most fundamental step in establishing the plan is insuring that all levels of the chain of command are functioning in their respective places before the plan is effected. This should not mean that the president of the corporation has to belabor the details of the plan; rather, it means that he will be involved in the basic decisions regarding the limits of the plan.

In the field of accounting, it is easy to see that top management rarely has the slightest notion of the limits of the plan. Once again, a subordinate department is charged with the detailing of a plan and proceeds to become the sole controlling factor. This particular weakness becomes most noticeable when an accounting change is made in the company. At such times the control and detail of the system are ordinarily within the confines of the accounting department itself, and no outsiders have any idea of what is expected or how the department functions. How many times will the president of an organization be obliged to shrug his shoulders, grin sheepishly and say, "Well, we better ask the people in accounting," when in fact he should be able to relate any alterations in accounting to his original plan. Compare this not uncommon condition with the simple plan for getting to work on time. In most cases working times are established by the top management of a company, and it would be ludicrous to imagine an executive vice president working out the detail of his employees' alarm clocks and their several traffic conditions. It would be just as absurd for an employee to change the company work hours for his own convenience. Yet this may very well be happening, in effect, in the company you work for now. As farfetched as it may seem, there are some firms that allow employees to set work hours for their own convenience, or companies in which the top management is so awed by the planning details, they allow various departments to set the priorities and capacities of the operation.

An example in point, the disaster of establishing independent schedules in an operating unit occurred in a large industrial plant north of Chicago. The production crane operators handling all the material took their first work break in the morning at 8:45. The maintenance crew which was responsible for changing the rollers on all critical equipment on a periodic basis took their work break at 9:00. Day after day, year after year, the maintenance crew is required to wait 15 minutes to change rollers on the milling machine while the crane operators take their break, after which time the maintenance operators go on their break. So literally, from 8:45 until around 9:20 every morning of production, all maintenance ceases in the production unit. In this particular instance, according to costing records, no plan at all had been established as to how long a roller change should take, the reporting consisted merely of documenting the time expended on roll changes. A quick calculation revealed that this same production plan was carrying an equivalent of twenty excess maintenance men. One simple synchronization problem had been caused by establishing a cross-chain of command break schedule. When the systems people interviewed all managers involved in the situation concerning the problem, instead of making the change immediately, a great deal of time was wasted as the various managers explained "that they had repeatedly instructed the maintenance people and the crane operators to work out relief breaks and not interrupt the roller changing in the process of taking their breaks." The irony of this particular case is that this same plan had no specified work break times spelled out in the bargain union contract. Therefore, management itself was solely and absolutely responsible for the addition of 20 people to the maintenance work load merely because they had failed to establish a plan, to keep it within the chain of command, to synchronize it and, thereby, to eliminate what had to be the most frustrating operation in the maintenance of that plant.

Once management understood the void created by its failure to detail the plan, it acted quickly to eliminate twenty $5.00 an hour employees. Roll changes in this plant now are changed on a fixed time goal basis, and management knows each and every time the cost exceeds the plan. This has netted that company a $200,000 annual reward.

ONE REMEDY

One method of getting all the personnel involved in the establishment of a plan is to review all of its elements. This method calls for simplification, not complication. Use the organization chart available for the basic levels of the chain of command. Jot down who does what and keep the flow simple. Remember, detailing of a plan is *not* the first step; recognizing the chain of command is, so be certain that chain is understood before proceeding.

CASE IN POINT

To illustrate how breaking the chain of command can destroy any planning, if it is not clearly communicated, we focus on a large construction company on the East Coast. In this particular instance, the construction company had experienced a loss of sales. In order to rectify this situation, the president demoted the general manager to sales manager until such time as sales came back up to their prior established level. In so doing, he had created a void in not filling the general manager's spot or appointing someone to fill the spot in the former manager's absence. The general manager, now sales manager, was a strong-willed individual and well respected throughout the organization.

In his new efforts to increase sales, he retained for himself all the prerogatives he had had as general manager. He still insisted on establishing and changing priorities. He even took it upon himself to assign project managers down to the foreman level on certain projects as they synchronized with sales. In so doing, he was bypassing the vice-president of construction. By the time the systems people were called in to help unravel the problems that were growing daily, the estimating department was acting independently of construction and the support areas of accounting, construction equipment, costing and purchasing. They also were unable to find what priority establishments or due dates were being required in the absence of the general manager. The systems people prepared an organization chart reflecting the situation as it existed at that moment and presented it to the president. The president, unaware of the havoc and friction in the various departments, failed to recognize that a clearly communicated, decision-making chain-of-command had to be established quickly in order to execute the plans that had been made into various operating levels. The construction vice-president no longer felt free to pre-assign key personnel at the project manager level to on-coming jobs. The project managers themselves would bypass the vice president of construction and call upon the new sales manager to determine what was their next assignment. This situation had permeated into all the areas and was going from bad to worse. The president, unaware of this situation and not wishing to have a confrontation with a temporary demotion at his top level, announced to the systems people that he, the president, would be acting general manager until such time as the sales manager moved back into the general manager's spot. It was not until the vice president of construction tendered his resignation, that the president was made acutely aware of what his indecision regarding the chain of command was doing to his organization.

MANAGEMENT BY EXCEPTION IN A CHAIN

When he recognized it, he quickly authorized the systems people to draft an organization chart showing the complete flow on chain of command. In addition, he authorized the systems people to work out a detailed step progress chart reflecting the flow from sales through estimating, to construction, to accounting, back to construction and the completion of a job. (See Diagram A) Once this had been completed, a firm plan was in place as to the priority and flow of sales and the interrelations between accounting and construction. While the diagram itself did not work out all the bugs that had been created with the personnel switch, it did give all the operating heads the ground rules under which they were to operate. In establishing this priority and flow diagram, the systems people were required to always have the organization chart on the wall in back of them as they walked each department head and then the department heads collectively through the flow. This construction company had been in existence very successfully for seventeen years and at no time had anyone in their organization taken time to draft an organization chart, establish the chain of command, get every department head and officer involved and work out the first basic step in setting up the plan—establish the chain of command.

Physical flow

The following routine represents the flow; responsibility patterns are set on this flow and must be adhered to for an orderly delivery.

(DIAGRAM A)

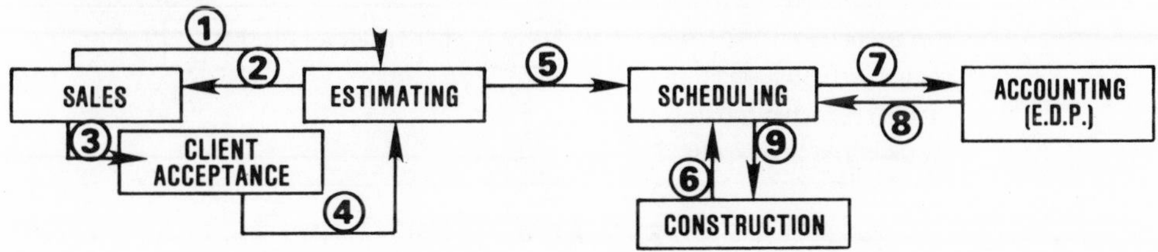

① Sales Department makes contact, requests a bid work-up.

② Bid work-up summary is delivered to sales department and presentation package is prepared.

③ Presentation is made to prospective client.

④ Upon acceptance and the signing of the contract, a request for a detailed estimate is generated by the sales department.

⑤ The detailed estimate is sent to scheduling when it is married to time frames.

⑥ The construction project manager supplies site and sequence information to scheduling. The result is the precedence diagram.

⑦ Scheduling sends the worksheets to accounting for E.D.P. processing.

⑧ The completed labor projection, schedule summary and audit lists are sent to scheduling for review.

⑨ Scheduling determines which releases to send to field and routes them to the project manager.

AVOID THIS PITFALL

Many excellent plans never get to the execution stage, let alone the control by exception phase, simply because the planner never worked out the detail of who is subordinate to whom at all levels (see Figure 4). In areas in which no top management plan exists, the first step must be to parade the new plan in its

Organization & Responsibility Chart

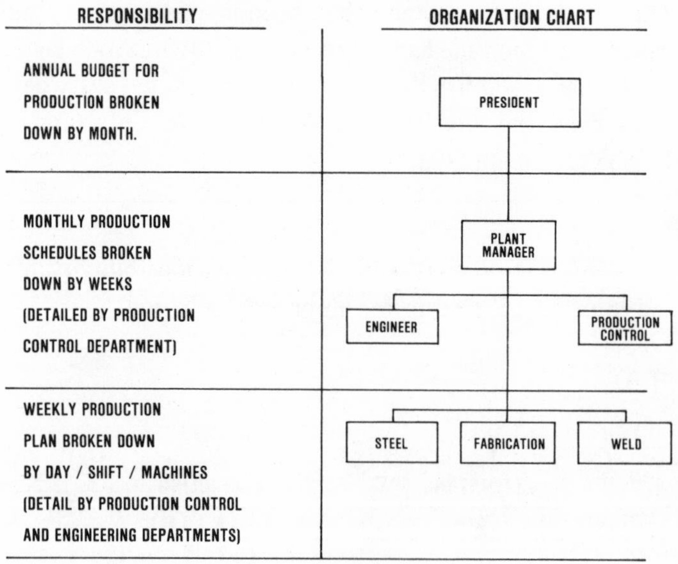

FIGURE 4

entirety before the top people so they have an opportunity to see it. It is not uncommon to find that some managers have sold themselves on the convenient concept of management control by evasion or exclusion and have been passing it off to their shareholders as Management by Exception.

A CLEAR-CUT CHAIN OF COMMAND

Many managers are opposed to (or so they state) showing their personnel in boxes, reporting to boxes underneath someone else. This is a complete abrogation of management's responsibility. In any inter-group activity in the business world, the more clearly a chain of command can be spelled out, the fewer problems you will have in the assignment of the detailing of a plan. Using the construction company once again as an example, we find the failure to spell out the top chain of command had caused considerable friction between the former general manager and the vice president of construction over assigning the foremen to the various projects. There was no recognition of the fact that both men were not entitled to assign foremen to the projects. The systems people, on this particular point, had taken the organization chart down to the foreman level. It became quickly apparent that the prerogative rested solely with the project manager himself and not with the vice president of construction or anyone else. It would be denying lower levels of command the ability to work the detail out of a plan for which they will be held accountable. The whole chain of command was implemented. The entire organization breathed a sigh of relief, for contrary to what many had believed, no one cared who assigned him as long as he knew who it was. A succinct chain of command could be quickly referred to and was easily available to everyone in the organization. Before the plan, there was much confusion as to who made assignments, and if the conclusions were valid. Therefore, the project manager had been bitterly opposed in the past to certain superintendents and foremen being assigned to his project. The failure to establish a chain of command in this particular company had resulted in an inability on the president's part to go down the chain of command and find exactly what was responsible for projects not being completed within a time frame or cost frame. Once the full system of Management by Exception had been established in this construction company, the president had the ability to follow down the chain of command and pin-point exactly which foreman on which project had failed on a certain day to do his part in delivering the overall plan.

By the end of the first year, after establishing the basics of a chain of command, this same president was able to show over $500,000 more profit than he had shown the year before. He, further, was written up in one of the construction industry's largest trade magazines in a feature story explaining how his company was "blossoming with tight personal management."

ESTABLISHING PRIORITIES AND RESPONSIBILITIES

This company, as many with similar problems, shows the surface results of failure to establish the chain of command in many different ways. One is constantly having to ask subordinate heads who is where, doing what or how well the individual is performing his assignment. Top management particularly bears the sole responsibility of establishing a chain of command. It can delegate working out the details of priorities and flow to and from various departments, thereby spelling out individual responsibilities. None of this can be accomplished if top management of a company is still operating under that old concept that individual employees will be dehumanized by showing them a priority and responsibility level chain of command.

Many classic examples exist in the business world of companies that have adopted the laissez faire method of delegating authority and ultimately end up with the inability to pinpoint the problems or failures of their corporations, as they sink from the business horizon. Thus, in the current recession, highly respected companies are failing to show a profit or a firm chance for survival. Look closely at many of these companies, particularly in the aerospace industry and you will detect immediately that "it was too complex" to establish a clear chain of command. How often employees at all levels in a company state, "I just don't know who I report to." At the same time, these same companies don't recognize what is causing the problem.

PINPOINTING EXCEPTIONS IN THE BUDGET

An example of this is seen in one major United States oil company, where a laborious method of department and top management budgeting takes place as it applies to gasoline, jet fuel, asphalt, wax and other product sales. This budgeting method, while difficult and detailed, has basically evolved into a guesstimate on the part of the person assigned, usually through percentage projections of what next year will look like. This particular company had enjoyed a consistent and healthy growth year after year from the end of the Second World War until the early '70's. The budgeting method was relied upon solely at the top management level as first proof that they were growing, and second, that all the subordinate levels of the chain of command were functioning smoothly. It was, in fact, a mirage. The annual budget itself was only reviewed once every quarter and then seldom, if ever, changed. What management failed to recognize is that the growth was a population and consumer expansion growth, and that they were in essence only enjoying their share of the market as they grew upward and onward, smug in the belief that their budgetary planning was what was making most of it happen. There had been no attempt in the entire planning mechanism to look at any exceptions whatsoever, and, furthermore, no attempt was made to know specifically where the budget was being executed, by what changes or what direct application of man-power. Management, therefore, had no conception of what to do, when for the second straight year their percentage increase budgetary projects failed to be met. The clerks extending last year's budget by percentage adjustments had no ability to offer any enlightenment to the puzzled higher levels of the chain of command. If such is the case in your company, your problem may be larger than merely the implementation of a Management Control by Exception System.

If such is not the case, however, a general review of all levels of command prior to the preparation of a plan will smooth the way for the next step, which is the execution of the plan. The review should place the responsibility for the plan's preparation on all shoulders and reveal to all that its execution is their collective responsibility.

CASE IN POINT

The all-purpose example of getting to work on time is pertinent here. A life insurance company headquartered for the past fifty years in downtown Los Angeles made the decision to move to an oceanside suburb to the south. The management of the company was involved in some extremely significant decisions regarding the work hours of the company at their new location. These decisions were made after detailed planning had been done by the systems people on the home locations of the clerical personnel, the freeway flows, local traffic to the beach and parking facilities. The president ultimately chose to initiate new office hours and to implement a six day/four day work week. Because of the new times, the employees would have to reset their alarms to arrive at work on time. This example suggests the responsibilities of the various levels of command when a plan is initiated for the first time. Unlikely as it may seem, the ''get to work on time'' plan did at one point involve all the levels of the company's management, though with considerable variance in attention to detail.

THE RELATIONSHIP BETWEEN PLANNING AND EXECUTION

It is probably safe to say that no top managers of an operation plan to give bad customer service. Yet, it seems that wherever he turns—in the grocery, the bank, at the airline ticket counter—the consumer is plagued by interminable lines. Why? Usually the reason is that some plan lacked the execution mechanism and consequently made exceptions the rule rather than merely one point of management control. Any plan must have the point of execution built in, or it will not be worth the effort it took to create it. The aerospace industry at its peak had whole departments glutted with people doing nothing but making plans for eventualities and probabilities, plans that would never be taken to the point of execution. The acres of empty parking lots in southern California are evidence of the failure of planning without execution. In order to measure the worth of any plan, it is absolutely necessary to take it to the point of execution. If the end result is execution, then it follows that when a top manager creates a plan and the next level in the chain of command details it further, that detailing is actually the next point of execution. The middle manager's details are further embellished by the line supervisor and subsequently assigned to an employee for implementation. This is a continuation of the plan-execute method of taking the original plan to the point of execution, which will ultimately result in correction and improvement of the plan. Any plans not designed to be taken to this point will never lend themselves to a truly workable Management Control by Exception system.

CASE IN POINT

One of America's largest corporations in the field of electronics allowed their public relations department to announce their coming prowess in the new field of electric automobiles. "Our firm is currently developing an over-the-road electric car!" True, some of their divisions had been developing component parts. But engineers developing component parts and a plan to assemble and de-bug these parts into an electric car was something else. The president of the company climbed on the bandwagon, and the resources of the company were hurriedly implemented toward putting out the publicity car. In great hast, the electric golf cart division put all the grand plans of the various divisions into a few prototype over-the-road electric cars. The entire episode was one designed and executed as an expedient, and no plans existed to manufacture and market an electric car. Once displayed, these autos of the future were quickly shelved. The president was pleased, the public relations department was off the hook and the prototypes rusted away. Had their management had a firm plan to execute, they might have had a very marketable item when the energy crisis hit five years later.

The basis for sending the exception back up the chain of command was missing and, thus, relegated any planning to the status quo, because of the lack of an improvement mechanism.

THREE EXAMPLES OF PLANNING

A. The grocery industry

Since most of us acquire early the habit of eating, the grocery industry will be a good place to begin. This industry offers some excellent examples of planning at all levels of management. In order to administrate a large supermarket chain, it becomes necessary to know what all the operating areas are doing without getting involved in the day to day detail of each store or warehouse. To accomplish this objective, the president of a large supermarket chain makes an overall plan for his entire operation. This plan is laid out on an annual basis by months. Each reporting division is measured against its past established performance, with current improvements taken into consideration. In the case of a Western grocery chain, the unit of measure is sales dollars per man hour. The president knows that the division in Las Vegas operates at a much higher dollar per man hour ratio than those in the metropolitan Los Angeles area, so, in fact, each division is planned according to its own history and field knowledge. This method of planning allows the top management of the company to agree or disagree with the plan before it is taken down to the field superintendent level. If the president doesn't like the results that the plan reflects, he is now in a position to shift his managers, advertising, capital equipment or any of the other means at his disposal to alter the plan for the desired results. Thus, while the overall plan for the entire corporation may be $30 per man hour, any given area may be different. Las Vegas, for instance, might be planned at $55 per man hour. Such planning must, of necessity, be detailed further before it can be executed and excepted at the cash register level.

There are several major grocery chains in this country in which the planning stops at the upper levels, and a yawning chasm exists between the overall plans of top management and the execution of the plan at the store level on an hourly basis. One notable example was a trading stamp company in Ohio that purchased a large grocery chain. The stamp company's top management had made very good plans to have their newly acquired group of supermarkets operate at $40 per man hour. However, they had made no provisions to take this excellent information to the next level of management for the purpose of detailing just how it could be executed at the store level. The systems people in this unhappy situation were told to "make improvements" within the confines of the master plan. The following year's annual report of the trading stamp company bemoaned the fact that, although operating improvements were being made . . . serious losses had been incurred in the newly acquired supermarket chain. Word on the street is that one can pick up this particular chain cheap.

Plans must be made so they can be detailed to the point of execution. The trading stamp company's supermarkets failed to do this and the results are just the opposite from those of the first cited grocery chain. In that latter chain, the president fully understood that the field superintendents would have to detail the plans as they applied to each of the various stores and operating areas. Further, the field superintendents knew that they too would have to allow the store and warehouse managers to detail their plans by intra-department areas and by days.

The plan of the president to operate the metropolitan Los Angeles division at $40 per man hour told the dollar volume anticipated, as well as the labor to be used. The metropolitan Los Angeles division manager knew that the store in the Watts area would operate at $30, while the Beverly Hills store would be at $58. The particular store manager then knew that he was going to expect sales of about $100,000 in a given week, and that his established performance was $40 per man hour, or a planned usage of 2,000 man hours to run the operation. The store manager was then free to spread his hours in the manner he knew best through the various days and departments, within the limits of the top management's plan. It should be emphasized here that the store manager *did not* make his own capacity establishing plan for the running of his operation. The decisions as to the performance dollar volume and manpower had been made while still allowing him to work out the details. Since an overall company increase of one dollar per man hour in sales amounted to $750,000 annually in less payroll in this particular chain, it is not difficult to see why the president told his shareholders of a $5,000,000 savings after the first nine months of using this approach.

B. Shoe manufacturing

In spite of the seemingly complex variations of the mix in the shoe industry, this same basic technique can be profitably applied there as well. The top manager of a shoe company which supplies Sears and Roebuck with its line of work shoes plans his whole year on the number of pairs of shoes he anticipates producing. This plan is broken down by computer to reflect the anticipated needs, styles, sizes and widths for the next twelve months. Such a breakdown allows management to make crewing and material adjustments prior to their commitment in order to level the work load between months and let the warehouse reflect the change in requirements. To maintain a constant work force once the plan has been initiated, each department head is charged with the responsibility of working out the detail of the work week for his section. In this particular shoe factory the computer, with all the individual employee's performance records and the multitudinous combinations of the steps, sizes, widths, and styles in its memory bank, works out the hourly detail of each day to insure a maximum output for the plant. In short, the computer, because of its calculating speed, details the president's plan at the point of execution. And this plant increased its output from 497,000 pairs in one year to 749,000 pairs the next, using the same number of people working on the same machines with the same basic product mix. The only element that changed was the detailing of a top management plan to the point of execution, the vital foundation for management control by exception system.

This shoe company paid all employees on a time incentive basis. Because of this an increase in shoe production reflected no savings in labor. Equally, since the raw materials for the increased production were also the same per pair of shoes, no dollar savings could be made there. Yet, the owner of this firm was most pleased with his additional $150,000 profit that year. As he explained it, "I just produced 300,000 pairs of shoes with absolutely no overhead on them!"

C. Bathtub fixtures

A company in Honolulu, Hawaii, manufactures fiberglass shower bathtub fixtures. Its costs were never certain, and since it was in a remote corner of the mainstream of manufacturing and also in a relatively new field, the company had almost no guidelines to go by. In one week there might be a cost of 18 man hours per unit, in the next that cost might be as low as 12. Needless to say, such instability played havoc with profits. The top man was more of a salesman than a manager, and while he had the ability to put the enterprise together, he found it all but impossible to operate at a profit.

The solution to his woes came when he implemented a system of Management Control by Exception. The first step, and to him the most difficult, was to sit down and lay out a simple manufacturing plan for the next three months. This difficulty was compounded in his case, since he had overrated the company's sales potential to his not-so-silent financial partners. He had avoided any sort of overall planning because it was foreign to him and, therefore, frightening, perhaps, because it made him come to grips with his actual sales requirements. In the meantime, his partners had employed some systems people to implement a system of Management by Exception that would allow them to review the operation and insure it was headed in the right direction. After the first overall plan had been made, and the production manager knew the actual requirements (for the first time, by the way), he was better able to utilize his personnel. The top management plan established 12 man hours per unit produced and set limits on the manpower which the production manager was authorized to employ. A detailed daily run was planned, and, when absenteeism or any other irregularities occurred, a unit was taken out of the reject storage, repaired and entered into the flow to offset the lost production. This procedure allowed the plant manager to attain his required units per day with his manpower under control. The operation now puts out the units at about 8-9 man hours per unit, for in addition to planning at the various levels of management, it added the element of the exception. This simple addition pointed the way to further improvement.

THE NECESSARY CORRELATION OF PLANNING AND EXCEPTION REPORTING

In the case of the fiberglass tubs, we have a telling example of marked improvement through the introduction of a planning element. From 18 man hours per unit to 12 is no small accomplishment.

This plant produced the same number of units the next 12 months as they had prior to the new system. What they didn't do was spend $30,960 in payroll the last 12 months due to improved productivity.

Similar results can be obtained in almost any operation in which the planning has been neglected, abandoned or desregarded. To retain the momentum of improvement and recap the added benefits, however, management must implement exception reporting. Exceptions will reveal to management not only that which they do not know, but the value or cost of that unknown as well. From such information comes a true increase in an operation's productivity.

Exception reporting has been described as nothing more than eliminating the lows and catching the highs. In Figure 5, we see an example of variations in

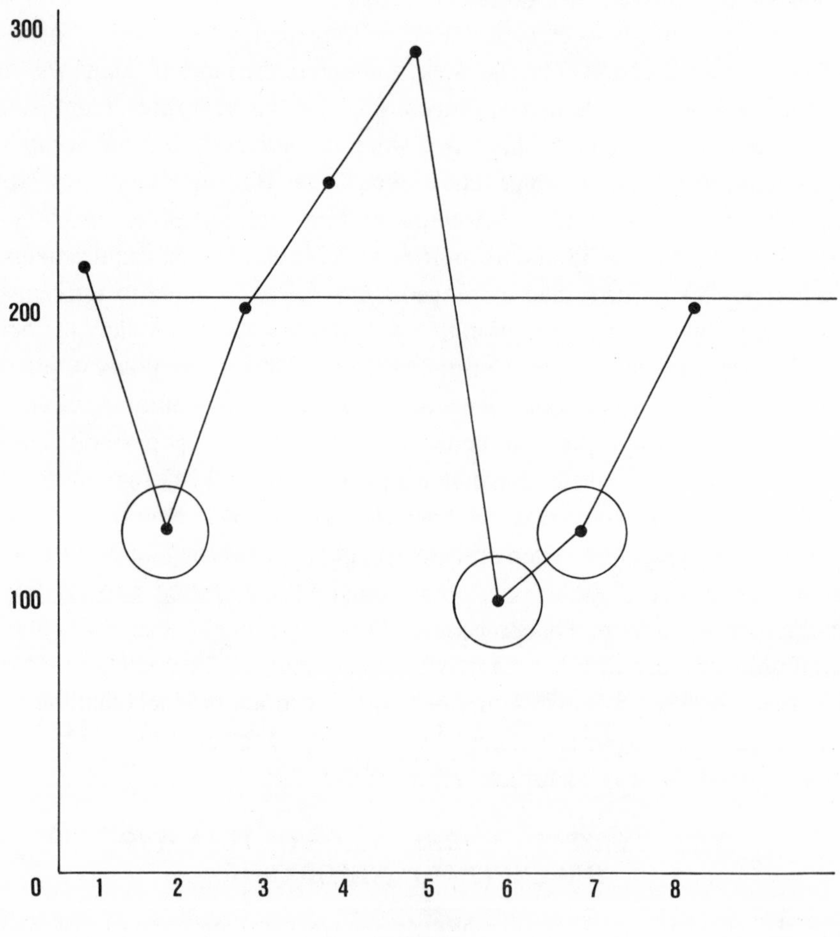

FIGURE 5

output. This example could be expressed in dollars, units, miles, pounds, tons or almost any unit of measure applicable to a given situation, but essentially what the figure shows is a variance in the daily performance. Once a plan has been made, these ups and downs become more pronounced; therefore, the more detailed the plan is next to the point of execution, the more specific becomes the identification of the variation. In the examples just cited, we could apply the figure to either a presidential report reflecting several months or to the operation on a daily basis reflecting several working days. At whatever level the plotting is made, the exceptions are still singled out; hence, the president can know he had three bad weeks, while the line supervisor may know he had three bad hours. This knowledge of when the plan was most excepted directs attention to the specific problem area. If we were going to control this particular operation by exception, we would now know where to look in order to initiate improvements. If, in Figure 5 as shown, the plan was made for 200, and we now know that three times we dropped to 100, we could then go about eliminating the problems identified. This process is possible only because we have laid out a plan in the first place and allowed a system of exception reporting to follow. It is the exception reporting that identifies the problems. All of this may appear elementary, but it is astonishing how many companies overlook it altogether.

FAILURE TO EMPLOY EXCEPTION REPORTING

Since the unfortunate truth is that exception reporting is not in general use, almost any industry or discipline within an industry (accounting, marketing, etc.) could be cited as an example for the lack of exception reporting. The surest sign that this element is missing is a manager—at whatever level, from president to department foreman—throwing up his hands in despair and exclaiming that he just can't understand what went wrong. Not infrequently, this will be the sad plight of the manager who is not using the element of exception: he simply doesn't know. To paraphrase the old joke about why a manager has round shoulders and sloped forehead, the answer is that when asked a question, he shrugs his shoulders and says, "Darned if I know . . ." and when shown the solution slaps his forehead and cries, "Why didn't I think of that?"

THE ANNUAL BUDGET: DOVETAILING PLANNING WITH EXCEPTION REPORTING

An annual budget provides what is probably the most obvious example of this problem. Whether it be the budget of a university or a zoo, such plans almost invariably reflect the absence of the exception reporting element. How often will companies spend untold hours preparing, then later approving the annual budget, only to shelve it and ignore the excesses committed thereafter in its name. Need one be reminded of that greatest of all annual budgets, the Federal budget. This is an excellent example of commitment to planning which is not at all related to exception reporting. When was the last time anyone mentioned the fact that in a particular month more billions were spent than were budgeted? The next year we pay the taxes for that little exception.

For some reason companies whose work is within the scope of the federal budget—that is, companies with government contracts—have an affinity for planning without exception reporting. In non-government work try charging more for your product than you originally contracted for, and you will no doubt see your last sale to that buyer. In some government contract industries, the reporting of every element is not only detailed but borders on the ludicrous. Yet these same companies never relate the budgets of their firms nor the plans of production to those endless reports. They merely record the fact, regardless of the plans themselves.

Many vendors in the realm of private industry, however, afford themselves this same luxury of failing to note and eliminate exceptions. The printing industry affords itself, at the customer's expense, the ability to over or under run the amount by 10%. Those users who depend on this type of delivery are condemned to eternal adjustments in inventory control, costing, production planning and the like. Think of ordering 5,000 of anything, having to wait for six to eight weeks and then having to plan to receive somewhere between 4,500 and 5,500 in inventory. Why? Because the vendor is simply inflicting his failures to use a simple Management Control by Exception onto the user.

CASE IN POINT: A

A major helicopter manufacturing company underwent a report purge and discovered literally tons of reports coming out of their twin IBM 360-65 computers each month. As they analyzed these reports, a dismal picture emerged. Not a single report included either the original plan or any relation to its exceptions. The reports offered an interminable stream of facts: today we produced 521089 widgets, 75444564 cluclus, etc. Splendid! But how many did we say we would produce? You can guess the answer: "Darned if I know." A tolerant systems man suggested kindly that it might be helpful to know the company was supposed to produce X number of widgets and Y of cluclus. And you know the rest: "Why didn't I think of that?" Another round shouldered, sloped forehead manager who never thought to relate his plan to exception reporting.

CASE IN POINT: B

A major airline headquartered in the Southwest holds a very precise, military-type briefing in its operations room each day. To attend these meetings is to be impressed indeed. The various representatives of the different departments all contribute their share to the briefing, and it proceeds like something out of a World War II movie. The meteorologist indicates the weather will be cloudy over Denver and that some turbulence is reported over Panama City. The head of operations tells which flights will be scratched. The other representatives perform their assigned functions. It all looks very good—dynamic planning. But that same airline has yet to hold a briefing over the failure of their plans to materialize. They plan intricately their flight schedules, but never report the exceptions of their flights, the late departures caused by exceptions on the ground. The result is that this particular airline has one of the highest safety records in the country and possibly the worst reputation for on time performance. They have very good plans, a dramatic method of communicating them, but not a single means in their entire system for relating exception reporting to those plans. Needless to add, the management of that airline has changed more than a few times in the past decade.

REVISING THE PLAN

If we return once more to the annual budget, we can see a good example of a plan that is never revised regardless of how ominously the future portends. Once made, the annual budget rests like the grail in some manager's (usually an accountant's) office, unchanged and unchallenged until time for its Lazarus-like revival the following year. If, for no other reason than the time expended on it alone, the annual budget should be paid more attention during the course of the year. It exemplifies a desperate need for feedback of the execution to the plan. If the time, effort and money that goes into the original preparation of the budget were diverted into revision of those golden thoughts as they are taken to the point of execution, and a revision made of all the planning that flows from the budget each month, what an improvement would occur!

Here, then, is one of the first and certainly one of the easiest methods of setting up and monitoring a system of Management Control by Exception: breathe life into your company's budget. The format is ready made. The plan ordinarily involves top management, and consequently, the authority required to implement any new system (or any changes in the existing one) is easily accessible. No basic changes in format or in original conclusions of the budget are needed. The only element missing is the report which feeds back information to the budget (that is, the top management fiscal plan) in the same manner in which it was created. Thus, if the budget is broken down monthly for each operating department, and if it is expressed in dollars, the report that must feed back into it should be expressed in the same terms, i.e., dollars per operating department per month. This axiom holds true for all aspects of the exception control system. That plan reported must be expressed in the same terms in which it was originally planned. Then, should the report reflect a noticeable variance from the plan, the first and most important exception has already been noted. This exception, while the most important, is also the least likely to be changed, since it is at the top of a pyramid of planning and feedback reporting and will lack any specific detail. A large variance between budget plan and budget report will almost always reflect a failure of the total underlying system.

A BASIC RULE

A fundamental rule to remember is that the larger the variance of the top plan when compared to the actual report, the more likely the basic system is not functioning at the subordinate levels. The very reason revision is so significant to Management Control by Exception is that, when major revisions are required, they point the way to noncompliance or misunderstanding somewhere in the subordinate levels of the system itself.

INFLEXIBLE PLANS, DINOSAURS AND OTHER EXTINCT SPECIES

When the budget is *not* changed, it is sure to be found waiting in the wings, ready to reveal the inadequacies of the top manager. If he brings his operation through the year "on budget," there is usually the lurking suspicion that it was either too easy in the first place or padded enough to be attained, regardless of the circumstances. On the other hand, failure to meet budget has been brought home to all of us in many ways, most of them financial, all of them painful: didn't meet the household budget, therefore had to borrow money; company didn't meet its budget, therefore no raise; company exceeds its budget, therefore stock doesn't do well and no dividends this year; increased costs not forseen in the Federal budget, therefore the tax bill is higher this year. And on and on. Plans must remain flexible and subject to change at the proper time, or they will fail to direct the operation properly and profitably. Dinosaurs became extinct because, in a changing environment, they failed to adapt. The first effects of the changing environment didn't wipe out the entire dinosaur population any more than a rigid plan will spell immediate doom for the operation employing it. Yet, the end result of both the dinosaur's demise and the operation's failure are equally inevitable.

CASE IN POINT

The management of a major grocery chain in Denver, Colorado, became increasingly alarmed at the loss of their customer service. Three years earlier they had hired one of the better known systems firms in the country to get them on a good, sound operating system. Among the many fine attributes of this system was the detailing of the number of checkers and checker helpers used in serving the customers. At the outset the new system paid handsome dividends in customer service, and sales were increased at the expense of other chains that failed to make similar change. After a time, however, it was noted that not only were the check-out lines lengthening, but there was also a subtle loss of dollar volume as well. In an effort to get at the root of the problem, management called in another systems group to analyze the situation.

The solution was found to lie in the store managers' detailing of the plan level. Plans for the check stands were not being changed from week to week; as a matter of fact, the managers were using the old plans rather than making new ones for each week, as the original system had prescribed. In one store, the original plan was found bordered in scotch tape to prevent the sheet from tearing—damaging evidence indeed of the inflexibility of the manager, for the tape itself was yellowing with age. The crewing at the check stands in this store had been the same, rain or shine, May or September. The store (and the chain as well) was now losing business in the same way it had taken it from its competitors. When a plan is never revised, serious trouble is surely in the offing.

SOME RULES FOR REPORTING

If it is necessary to revise a plan, and, if the means of identifying when a revision is needed varies from the plan, then it is the report that must carry the responsibility for the required revision. An effective report in a Management Control by Exception System must have certain rules in place. The first is that the report must bear a memorandum of the plan. Next, it must include a method of reflecting actual performance so that comparison with the plan is possible with no further information needed. The report must also be timely, accurate and meaningful, in addition to having the plan and its execution in comparative positions. A copy of the plan itself, with the blanks for the execution attached, may be sufficient when filled out to make an excellent report. In practice, a good report rarely needs to be anything more than an updated comparison of the plan with the actual performance.

In Figure 6, the plan is a line graph which could represent hours of machine running time, loading time, or almost any plan desired. It is particularly useful in situations in which synchronization between pieces of equipment is important, or in which a visual plan is helpful for the operators. By simply opening up the plan line to allow the entry of the actual execution of the event, the ever necessary comparison has been made on the plan, thus forming a reporting receptacle. This basic illustration may suggest how easy it is to open up the annual budget in exactly the same manner. The only difference is that in the annual budget one is dealing with numbers instead of colored lines or X marks. Figure 7 shows a typical annual budget and its use as a comparison of a plan and actual performance.

Line Graph Representing Plan Time

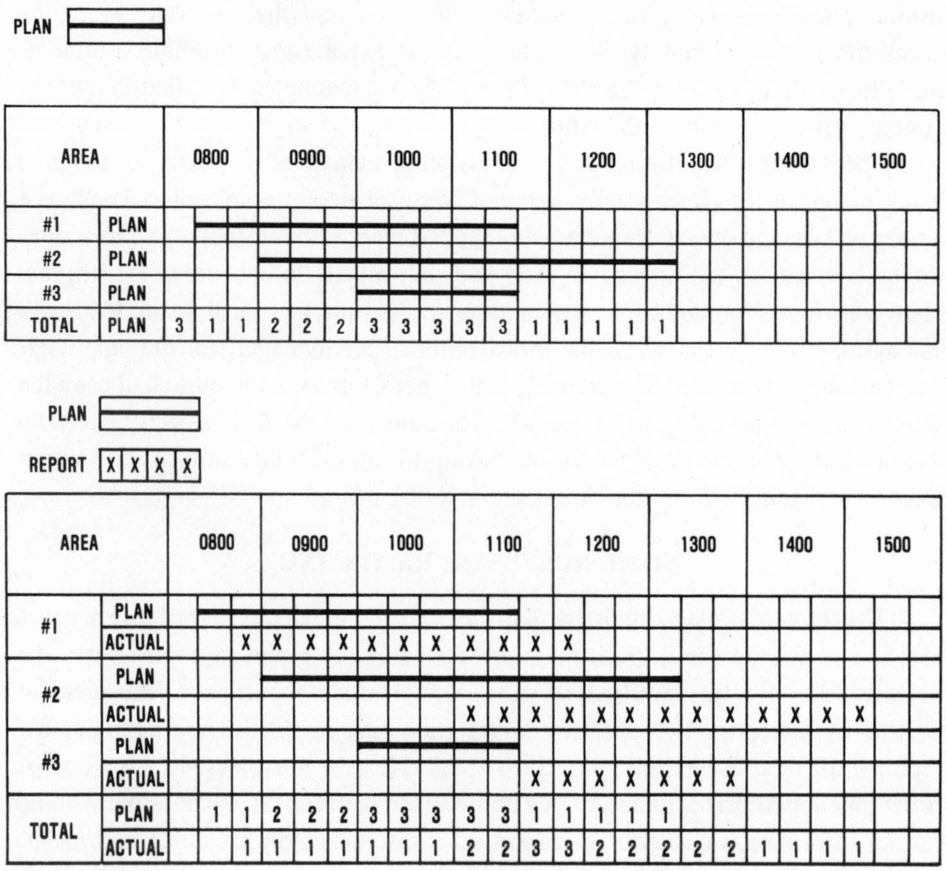

PLAN

AREA		0800			0900			1000			1100			1200			1300			1400			1500		
#1	PLAN																								
#2	PLAN																								
#3	PLAN																								
TOTAL	PLAN	3	1	1	2	2	2	3	3	3	3	3	1	1	1	1	1								

PLAN

REPORT X X X X

AREA		0800			0900			1000			1100			1200			1300			1400			1500		
#1	PLAN																								
	ACTUAL			X	X	X	X	X	X	X	X	X	X	X											
#2	PLAN																								
	ACTUAL										X	X	X	X	X	X	X	X	X	X	X	X	X		
#3	PLAN																								
	ACTUAL												X	X	X	X	X	X	X						
TOTAL	PLAN		1	1	2	2	2	3	3	3	3	3	1	1	1	1	1								
	ACTUAL			1	1	1	1	1	1	1	2	2	3	3	2	2	2	2	2	1	1	1	1		

FIGURE 6

Plan **19— Budget**

Area	*January*	*February*	*March*	*April*	*May*	*June*	*July*	*August*	*September*	*October*	*November*	*December*
A	1000	1000	1000	1000	1000	1000	1000	1000	1000	1000	1000	1000
B	750	750	750	750	750	750	750	750	750	750	750	750
C	800	800	800	800	800	800	800	800	800	800	800	800
Total	2550	2550	2550	2550	2550	2550	2550	2550	2550	2550	2550	2550

Actual **19— Budget**

Area		*January*	*February*	*March*	*April*	*May*	*June*	*July*	*August*	*September*	*October*	*November*	*December*
A	*Budget*	1000	1000	1000	1000	1000	1000	1000	1000	1000	1000	1000	1000
	Actual	1000	800	750									
B	*Budget*	750	750	750	750	750	750	750	750	750	750	750	750
	Actual	200	500	500									
C	*Budget*	800	800	800	800	800	800	800	800	800	800	800	800
	Actual	1000	800	800									
Total	*Budget*	2550	2550	2550	2550	2550	2550	2550	2550	2550	2550	2550	2550
	Actual	2200	2100	2050									

FIGURE 7

AN EXAMPLE OF THE PLAN REPORT RELATIONSHIP

While an annual budget is an overall top management plan and therefore must have the information fed into it in the same manner as it was prepared, it must be remembered that the plan-report relationship has to be maintained throughout the entire system. Thus, if a department head is charged with the responsibility of preparing a monthly plan for his area from the annual budget and detailing it so that his section heads can prepare their weekly plan, then it follows that the department head must have a report that will compare on a monthly basis with his plan.

In Figure 8 an example of a clerical plan for a month is shown. This plan has

Clerical Plan for a Month

ITEM	CLERICAL WORK LOAD																			
	M	T	W	T	F	M	T	W	T	F	M	T	W	T	F	M	T	W	T	F
REPORT A	O	—	—	—	×															
REPORT B						O	—	—	—	×										

ITEM	CLERICAL WORK LOAD																			
	M	T	W	T	F	M	T	W	T	F	M	T	W	T	F	M	T	W	T	F
REPORT A	●	—	—	—	⊗															
REPORT B						O	—	●	—	×	⊗									

O = MATERIAL AVAILABLE

× = REPORT DUE

● = MATERIAL RECEIVED

⊗ = REPORT COMPLETED

FIGURE 8

been detailed to reflect the major work flow through the department for that month. Here, the volume is not as important to the manager as the start and finish times of the various reports (these will include accounting as well as production reports). The major emphasis of this plan-reporting system is on the exceptions of the department in both the input as well as the output. The ability of any department head to call his shots on the delivery of the finished product will be one of the major elements of evaluation. In this type of plan-reporting, the manager can look at his own score and can also know where the trouble spots are brewing.

HOW TO MAKE A REPORT PROVIDE FOR THE DETAIL OF EXCEPTIONS

If a report includes the plan (in whatever form, from a detailed numerical configuration to a simple stick graph) and a recording of the actual performance, the detail of the exception has already been implied. In Figures 6, 7 and 8, the variation between the plan and the performance suggests immediately the areas of exceptions. Their detail will be found in the line level execution point. (Specific reasons and causes categorized for top management solution are covered in the following chapters.) For now, we need only realize that whenever a plan is counterbalanced with the report of the execution, that report has provided for the detail of the exception.

In Figure 6 the exceptions are spelled out in the variances of the lines, both in clock time as well as in duration. These are expressed both graphically in the body of the plan-report and numerically in the summation at the bottom. As a firm's drive against exceptions increases, the necessity for detailing the variances becomes more important, and provisions must be made in designing a system to allow the reasons to be collected and grouped for the attention of management.

HOW TO AVOID REPORTING THE UNIMPORTANT

The first essentials in any system reporting are the proper consideration of the audience and the purpose the report will serve. What is excessive detail for one level of management is vital data for another. By matching the report with the plan, one can ordinarily avoid reporting excessively cumbersome and useless detail. *The report should never be more detailed than the executed plan it is reporting*. A simple method in the evaluation of reporting as it applies to the user is to have the user explain the report itself to you. Almost always managers in a straight-forward manner will pick up the report and show you what is meaningful to them and explain it. Many times the manager will circle only one figure and say, "This is all I ever look at on this report." This is not an isolated extreme, but rather, the rule. Examples of this may be quickly found where disciplines are being crossed, such as a laborious accounting report coming off the computer 3 inches thick and being sent to the marketing manager or the production manager. A quick interview with the production manager will reveal that he makes no attempt to look at any of the 3 inches save the conclusion line which tells him his variance of manufacturing standards. The report itself may be expressed in the accounting discipline for it is relatively meaningless to him, and he has no desire to receive it. He can't use it once received, and it continues to lay up expenses and consume space in his office. The oft quoted fact that good managers use the bottom line of a report to draw conclusions is nothing more than another way of stating that the detail of the execution is relatively unimportant to a manager, unless it is not happening as planned.

If no plan existed in the first place, then he merely wants to know the conclusion of the laborious report. Prior to implementing any Management by Exception System, a complete and thorough purge of false reports, over reporting, redundant and repetitive reporting should be eliminated from the operation.

REPORTING SYSTEMS IN PRODUCTION

An easy example of this type of reporting can be found in a production plant, where the employees themselves account for the time spent against various products. These initial employee oriented cards showing a total absence of any plan are then key punched, computerized, placed into the memory of a very expensive computer and extracted in dozens of different formats, all based on the same unplanned information being tallied at the employee level. Reviewing the reporting system of a manufacturing plant in Dayton, Ohio, the management systems manager was explaining how many reports were in existence in his plant showing the level of production, and how well management was controlling. It read like a dictionary of reporting. There was a standard cost report, the machine report, the cost per hour report and so on. The simple fact was that all these reports were merely another way of looking at the employee cost code related time cards being prepared in the absence of a plan, whereby each employee in the production unit was required to place all his hours against one or more pieces of production. One need not be a systems man to guess that the employees accurately accounted for every hour for which they were paid, regardless of the happenstance of the production at the time.

The reporting system itself was not only meaningless, it was false. It was parading as a management system, whereby management could call for any one's view in the production unit to tell them how it was functioning. It was in essence an exercise in long division in seven or eight different ways. World almanacs are a collection of sterile reporting of the unimportant. They are neither timely, accurate or particularly meaningful to the individuals reading them. The almanac is, in fact, a collection of interesting information and statistical information. The reason few people get excited about reading the *World Almanac* is that it was not their plan being executed or a report of such, but is, in essence, a sterile reporting of happenings upon which they had no influence or control.

KEY QUESTION

The question must then be asked by any systems man, "How much world almanac reporting is in existence in this company today that will stand in the way of a truly accurate, timely, meaningful report to the managers, who must use it as a mechanism to improvement by eliminating the exceptions?"

If a president uses a total volume, manpower and performance plan with monthly increments, the corresponding report should reflect this same information, even though that information may be on a weekly basis. In an organization in which the president requires such a report, it might be necessary for the foreman on the production line to compile the hours and incidents of the production. All management levels between these two extremes should include details sufficient to the extent of their individual plans. It should be added, here, that many papers masquerading as bonafide reports circulate through companies, when, in fact, they are no such things.

THE FIRST QUESTION

The first question a systems analyst must ask of a piece of paper glutted with detailed information is—why does this exist? Once this question is asked, it will be discovered that the only valid reports are those relevant to a plan prepared earlier. Reports are nothing more than messengers carrying the results of the executed plan to the plan maker. At this juncture, it must be born in mind that in ancient Persia the bearer of bad tidings was executed. While the attempt to bury the system which reports bad news will be initially attempted on the insertion of the Management by Exception Reporting System, one must remember that the messenger almost always had no influence on the report. Many times at the inception of a new exception reporting system that requires all levels of management to firmly face the facts of failure or lost productivity, an outcry will immediately come up that the system itself is causing these problems. The implement of this system must be prepared to meet this challenge by reemphasizing that the messenger himself did not fight the battle, he only delivered the results. With this guideline in mind, you will soon be able to discriminate between false and authentic reports. Random bits of information may be useful to the operation of a company, but unless they are directly relevant to the plan, they may be invariably classified as memoranda or records.

SCREENING OUT UNNECESSARY TECHNICAL REPORTING

Both memoranda and records are essential for the operation of a company, but they are hardly the vital pulse of management's plans in action. They have their place, but it is not at the top of the president's morning work pile, nor should they have priority at other levels of management in a company. Rather, they should rest in the libraries and repositorires of the technician, not the manager. An example of this type of reporting could be found on a large sugar plantation on the island of Hawaii. It had been the custom for years to have the top plantation manager be an absolute expert in the details of cane production. This, in turn, had led to units of measure and memorandum type reporting which he could point to with pride. Tons of cane per acre became the culmination of this reporting system. When a large Canadian firm purchased the holding of the plantation, the plantation manager found himself in conflict with his Canadian managers. They couldn't have cared less about the tons of cane per acre and explained to him that they were in the business of producing dollars per acre. In his attempt to increase the tonnage, he had also increased his fertilizer, water, and labor costs beyond the point of profitability. He was a hero in the Hawaiian islands for his tons per acre, but his job was in jeopardy with his new Canadian management, for he had failed to keep sight on dollar profit per acre. This is an example of technical reporting which can become so detailed and laborious that it closes management's eyes to that which they are there to plan. The only successful way to avoid the unimportant is to screen it out before it becomes entrenched in the "reporting" system. The helicopter firm cited earlier is more typical than not of companies that flood themselves with information in the form of unimportant data, simply because they fail to weed out that which is insignificant.

A RULE OF THUMB

An effective systems man must always remember that, if an information sheet has no plan prepared before it, then it can't be a report. Furthermore, if the detail of the authentic report includes more information than was required to prepare the plan, it belongs to whatever level of planning that needs and uses that much information.

COLLECTING THE UNRELATED PIECES

Just as we must avoid the unimportant in reporting, so also must we be certain we are collecting the unrelated pieces of information. The best means of doing so is to make sure the planning has included a provision for contingencies. Often one hears managers say they couldn't plan for the unexpected. How revealing such a complaint is! One wonders why such managers think they need a system in the first place. The very purpose of a system is to prepare as much for blustery waves as smooth waters. In fact, if the sailing is all that smooth, one might well question the purpose of a good system at all. The irregular and the unexpected are the fundamental rationale for management in the first place. If this is true, then unrelated pieces of any system are clues to potential solutions to problems.

CASE IN POINT

A large firm engaged in warehousing, trucking and retail and wholesale grocery selling moved to reduce the price of the items offered for sale in its retail outlets. The plan-reporting system reflected various units of measure for the various entities. The warehouses used cases shipped, the stores' dollars sold, and the trucks' tonnage. In contrast to the past year, sales in the retail outlets were down by about 6 per cent. This downward trend seemed to be the pattern in the entire market that particular year and most managers in the grocery business attributed it to an economic slump and let it go at that. But the manager of this operation had a Management by Exception system in place and he was unwilling to accept this easy answer. The seemingly unrelated movement of cases in the warehouse and the dollars in the store led him to a more realistic and valid conclusion than that arrived at by his competitors. His cases shipped out of the warehouses showed a 10 per cent *increase* over the same period of time the previous year, and his major customers from those warehouses were his own retail stores.

Once these apparently unrelated pieces of information were collected, the president called for the plan-report of the next level in his chain of command in order to review the detail of the information. The detailing of what was being shipped soon reflected the fact that, while dollar sales were down, the work output at the store levels was up. The economic conditions that had cut back on spending had not correspondingly cut back eating. In fact, the better known, more expensive brands showed a marked decrease while the less expensive house brands were increasing. The net result was that more cases of goods were being sold while the dollar sales were, at the same time, slipping. If provisions for seemingly unrelated items had not been made in the planning-reporting of this operation, such information would have been lost to the president, even as it was lost on his competitors. This case in point—the president was receiving different conclusion information from the dollar amount and the cases being sold. The tonnage of the trucks verified the accuracy of the case count and the deception of the dollar amount. Therefore, reporting in and of itself, many times, will be dependent for audit on a cross discipline report which focuses back on the same basic items.

FEEDING THE PLAN INTO THE REPORT

While the report must always reflect the plan as well as its execution, there may be times when it is necessary to include some particular item in the planning because of the method of reporting. This will become even more common as industry moves to more systems automation. An example of what this implies is the impulsing of order requirements into the computer through the use of an adding machine or a telephone. Here it is necessary to adapt the planning format to the reporting result required, so that the computer cannot only accept the information, but can print it out in a manner comprehensible to the user. When a reporting system is being fed from many and various departments or operations, the top management report may require bits of information from each of the several reporting areas. This information must be placed into the planning as a direct result of its need in the top management report.

CASE IN POINT

A good example of this procedure is an item that changes units of measure as it passes through the flow. In a printing company orders enter the flow as sales dollars and units of finished product, yet in traveling through the plant the units of measure are not in those terms at all. In the web press department the unit of measure might be impressions, while in the composition department the units are expressed as plates, lines or galleys. The bindery, on the other hand, uses the unit of measure called signatures. In order to feed all this variation into a single management reporting system, it is necessary for the departments to express their volumes in terms of equivalent books or standard hours of production. In such cases planning has to be set up to feed into the reporting scheme. In operations even more complex or diverse, this common language or modification of the planning becomes all the more important. This particular aspect of setting up and monitoring a system of Management by Exception is easier to understand if one remembers that the very complexity or diversity of the system has dictated its need in the first place. Once a workable system is established, however, the end result is to make the entire operation easier to understand and, consequently, easier to improve. Oftentimes, improvement has not been achieved simply because the top management or the systems designer never backed into the planning after the reporting was operative.

METHODS OF IMPLEMENTATION

It is always unwise to over-complicate the methods of implementation. They are really rather simple if one never forgets their basic rules and refuses to be diverted from the main purpose: setting up and monitoring a system of Management by Exception. As some wit once put it, "When you're up to your waist in alligators, it's hard to remember the reason you're there is to drain the swamp." The following are three basic rules of implementation:

1. A plan must be established at all levels of the chain of command. The detail of the plan must be increased until the plan is taken to the point of execution.
2. Each plan must have a report. For each level of the chain of command, a report should exist. Reports must reflect a comparison of the plan to the execution of that plan, and they should have less detail as they move up the chain of command.
3. Variances must be noted on the report itself. They must be grouped and collected as they move up the chain of command for purposes of overall identification of the real problem areas.

In the implementation of a system of Management by Exception, one should use whatever practicable pieces of system are already in place. Creating a system from the bottom up is at best difficult, and, unless the top management is sold on the benefits that will accrue from the implementation of the full system, it becomes hard to obtain the necessary cooperation of all concerned. Further, it is not always necessary to "re-invent the wheel" merely because you find you need one. A careful analysis of the system currently in use will save you a great deal of grief. Most systems of Management by Exception are half in place when you begin. Those that have been successfully implemented are usually those in which the implement recognized the fact from the start.

MANAGEMENT BY EXCEPTION POINTERS

1. The first rule of Management by Exception is that a plan must be established at all levels of the chain of command. This plan will ordinarily consist of both historical information and field knowledge.
2. If the plan is to be effective in practice, all levels of the chain of command must be observed.
3. All elements of the proposed plan should be carefully reviewed before the plan is implemented.
4. When the exception becomes the rule, then the fundamental relationship between planning and execution has failed.
5. Exception reporting will reveal discrepencies *only* when the plan is established and executed. The function of the exception report is to identify problems as they arise in the execution of the plan.
6. Revisions to the plan must be made as the exceptions are noted and reported. If a plan is rigid and inflexible, exception reporting can do nothing to remedy operational problems.

7. Effective reports should include a memorandum of the plan and a comparison of that plan with actual performance. In this way variances can be noted on the report. It goes without saying the report should also be timely and accurate.
8. The report writer should always consider both his audience and the purpose his report will serve. The amount of detail will always depend on the management level reading the report. It is generally true that as those levels rise, the detail will decrease commensurately.
9. The report must never be more detailed than the executed plan being reported upon.
10. The systems analyst should always ask of any document—why does this exist?
11. Apparently unrelated bits of information may, when collected, provide clues for potential solutions to operational problems.
12. In reporting highly complex operations, it may be necessary to convert the variant units of measure into common terms.

3

ACTION AND DOCUMENTATION: CRITICAL KEYS TO SUCCESSFUL MANAGEMENT BY EXCEPTION

UNRECORDED ACTIONS AND THEIR EFFECTS

Unless the employee is provided with a method of recording exceptions at the initial point of a plan's execution, any action taken to make the plan succeed will be taken without the knowledge of the planner. This simple fact suggests many interesting consequences when you remember that today's executed plan is likely to be the blueprint for tomorrow's new plan. Unrecorded actions will frequently go undetected by management for the entire course of an operation, and it is conceivable that such actions might never be known but for the seemingly inevitable intrusion of a new manager or employee or a change in physical location of the new operation. Such intrusions—if they can be termed that—bring to light the previously unrecorded action, often with devastating effect.

CASE IN POINT

One of the most menial work assignments is the folding of the industrial wipe towels into flat stacks of ten and the subsequent tying of ten such stacks into bundles of a hundred. The pace is constant, the activity routine to the point of maddening frustration and the work unvaried in content. Simply put, line procedure is continuously repeated until the specified work period has elapsed. Needless to say, the ideal employee for this type of operation would be drawn from the ranks of the mentally disadvantaged. Like so much low level or "stoop" labor, it is among the last to be successfully automated. What this means is that managers of industrial laundries are not looking at new equipment to phase this tedious operation out of existence. It should follow, then, that this would be one area of management in which all the details could be worked out, one in which a systems man could not possibly find any exceptions.

However, a closer examination reveals that just the opposite tends to be the case. Towel folding is a job that appears to defy change or challenge, and management has almost no means of recording those little actions that might point to improvement. An industrial laundry in Pennsylvania had such an operation; it employed twelve people to fold and bundle the towels that it laundered and served to the local industrial market. During the course of developing a system for this plant, it was noted that, whenever a delay occurred between the drying machine and the folding table, the folders would reach under the table, pull up a ten fold hundred piece bundle, break it open and scatter the contents on the very table upon which the bundle had been folded before. This practice was particularly interesting in view of the fact that the folding operation was paid on a piece incentive basis. When the plant manager was asked why his people did this, he replied, "Those morons have run out of work, and they think they're fooling me." Apparently it had never occurred to him that, when he set up the crewing for the plant each week, he was including that known—but unrecorded—fact in his estimate. A recording of the output on an hourly basis quickly reflected the rather alarming fact that the individual output of the employees in this operation varied by well over 100%. One hour an employee might fold and bundle 28 bundles, yet the very next hour his performance could drop to as low as 11.

HOW THE PLANNER GOT OFF THE TRACK

The above illustration exemplifies unrecorded actions that were known, yet somehow escaped the attention of the planner. Because this particular plant manager was looking at the daily output of the department, he saw no noticeable variance in the performance of the towel department. His amusement at the attempts of his workers to appear busy had blinded him to the central issue which was, indeed, before his very eyes. The employees were, in fact, running out of work on a routine basis. By using the department's performance to determine next week's crewing, the manager built the unrecorded action into the schedule again.

Thus, the task itself was not only menial and monotonous, but the failure of the planner to eliminate a loss of materials with which to work had added yet another frustration to the job and condemned the employees to an even lower pay scale.

This particular case, has, however, a happy ending. Professional systems personnel implemented a system of Management by Exception, and as their initial step they began recording the output of the department by each hour. Next, the plant manager was trained to look for variations of that output as his first indicator of unrecorded actions that might be hindering his productivity. Through such training he was able to solve the flow bottleneck, eliminate certain stoppages and reap the benefits of knowing precisely the actions his people were taking to institute a better plan. At that time the national average for folding these towels was 20/22 bundles per hour. By recording actions now known or accounted for in the past, the plant manager now was taking action on the exceptions and eliminating them. At last check this same plant was maintaining an average of 32/34 bundles per hour, and, naturally, costs dropped commensurately.

Since the plant manager saw he no longer needed a crew of 12 to do the work and since he did appreciate his employees, he turned the savings into additional production. He now proceeded to take business away from his competitiors in order to fill his new found capacity. He could do this because, though he paid his workers 50% more each for the increased output, he didn't have to raise his prices for the next three years, while his competitors did. After all, labor was only 20% of his price. This increased business yielded a $75,000 greater profit from towels alone in the first year. And remember, this was after a 50% pay increase had been paid. Absenteeism was very low in that plant for some time.

AVOIDING THE ACTION THAT ELUDES DETECTION

Oftentimes, a plan for an operation grows out of past failures that have not been adequately worked out; consequently, the plan in action is not always the best for the operation but is simply the easiest to execute with regularity. Planning of this sort tends to be self-perpetuating, due to the inability of the management to detect the real reasons for the irregularities.

CASE IN POINT

The employer of a service operation had sixteen delivery trucks covering the entire city. Every afternoon the trucks returned to the plant anywhere from three to six p.m., on an average, though sometimes in bad weather or holiday traffic the first trucks would not arrive until as late as eight p.m. A crew of unsupervised employees were left in the plant to unload the trucks in preparation for the loading the next morning. Because of the irregularity of the truck arrivals and the employees' desire to earn more money (after five p.m., the unloading was done on overtime), this company was paying an average of $15 in wages to unload each truck. When the work content was calculated by a local industrial engineer, the cost came to less than $3 per truck at the same labor rate.

IDENTIFYING SOURCES OF COST OVER-RUNS

This is a particularly apt example of ''planning'' that avoids taking into account the action that eludes detection. In this case the employer was ''working around'' or ''living with'' the troublesome and expensive action, rather than determining in advance that costs were out of control and demanding some accounting for those exorbitant costs. The solution for this problem was discovered by the industrial engineer, who presented management with the brutal fact that they were spending 500% more than was necessary to get the job done. He had, in fact, placed the problem in focus by identifying the cost and the avoidance. In cases such as this, management avoids that action which would solve the problem because, in truth, they have been unable to detect the action which is the real cause of the problem. The unloading quandary was resolved by bringing in the crew at five a.m. and making available all of the trucks as well as the known work load on hand. Thus, management was able to supervise the work in much the same manner the towel folders were supervised. The format employed is quite simple and is most effective in documenting work flow interruptions (see Figure 9).

	Time Periods					
Cause	8/10	10/12	12/2	2/4	4/6	6/8
Equipment Break Down						
No Work Available						
Parts Not Available						
Wrong Information						
Interruption						
Training Required						
No Assignment Given						
Insufficient Volume						
Site Conditions						
System Non-Complete						
Totals						

FIGURE 9

By knowing in advance what the work should be and by documenting the reasons for the exceptions, actions can no longer go undetected and the manager is able then to create a more effective plan.

PLANNING WITHOUT THE FACTS

Perhaps the best known and most obvious illustration of action taken with the planner ignorant of the facts is that of the boy allowed by his parents to sell Kool-Aid on the corner some hot summer afternoon. Once the boy begins to make money and achieve a small measure of success, his enthusiasm is likely to push him on to greater ambition. Given another hot day, he is ready to return to his corner and get to business again. It is at this point the young manager will likely have to face facts he has been unaware of before. His mother, for example, may ask him where he plans to get the Kool-Aid mix and possibly even the sweetner and the cups. The first time around, he was no doubt furnished with all of these necessities and, in effect, was allowed to take actions of which he, as manager, was ignorant. Now, if he hopes to perpetuate his business success, more specific planning will have to take place.

This example may appear too simple, but it is analogous to problems repeated daily in almost any industry one can name. A new sales manager will take over a company and issue orders regarding a new sales approach. Following the institution of his new policy, sales in certain areas may reflect an increase very shortly. Flushed with confidence, the manager redoubles his efforts in those directions, but somehow his initial successes are never repeated. He calls another sales meeting and discovers, to his chagrin, that the spurt of sales was in fact caused by some effort in flow long before he took charge or by a regional economic situation temporarily favorable, and that his "revolutionary" approach was not even used at the time of the increase. In cases of this sort, the planner is ignorant of all the relevant facts, and he proceeds on the erroneous assumption that his plan has insured success. Sales are cited here, since so many sales managers are currently looking for work, largely because of this single inability to apply the dual elements of managing by exception: action and documentation of the action.

CASE IN POINT

The examples of this costly sort of ingnorance are legendary. They range from the complex computerized production control releasing method of a major farm implement company to the simple releasing method employed by a smaller manufacturing firm. In both cases the plan as issued was impossible to produce, since the necessary parts were simply not available. Yet somehow, miraculously, the production schedules were obtained. When both of these companies called in professional systems personnel trained in the use and application of Management by Exception, a parts check sheet was prepared, and orders were not issued until the parts could be located. Once the production orders were traced in the plants, it was discovered, in each of these cases, that the foremen were keeping "kitties" or parts hidden in order to make the schedules as issued.

The solution lay in the return of all fittings to the supply departments. Records, for example, might reflect ten thousand 2" cotter pins available, but the supply department issued the entire box of pins to the first foreman requesting them. This in turn gave the receiving foreman his "kitty" to trade with another foreman who might come up short for the part. The original production order might have called for two thousand of the pins. The records in the computer or kardex file reflected first a consumption of the two thousand pins and thus a remainder of eight thousand. The problem, however, was that no one could find the pins without asking someone at the production line level. Sad to say, this rather devious trading method of foremen in most manufacturing plants is more the rule than the exception. The systems people instituted tighter controls of the release of parts from the supply department. Specific amounts were issued to various departments, but only as called for by the production orders. Such action required the addition of several men to the supply parts department in order to count and weigh the parts, but there was a corresponding reduction in personnel in the assembly departments, as they no longer had to wait while their foremen sought to trade or "expedite" their parts.

THE RESULTS OF ACTIONS WITHOUT DOCUMENTATION

Picture an employee having to kick his machine to get it started or to keep it functioning properly, and you have a visual image of action taken without documentation. As long as the kicker is on the job, the machine will function; if he is absent, or if he leaves, management may well be faced with a non-productive piece of equipment until someone discovers the kicking secret, or until the machine is properly repaired. Because the employee who kicked the machine had no method of documentation, management cannot evaluate or remedy this particular situation. Without such documentation there can be no guarantee the situation will not recur, the employee's verbal instructions notwithstanding.

CASE IN POINT

A well known medical laboratory has a small plastics plant in California in which the machines run around the clock, seven days a week. Before the installation of an exception reporting system, management was unaware that over half of the employees sevicing the front end of the plastic extruding equipment had no notion whatsoever of how to do the job; nor had there been any method of documenting the production losses or variances in hourly production. Unlike the raw materials in most manufacturing operations, plastic can be ground up and used again. Where no system of exception reporting exists, the scrap or back production sits in the plants as mute evidence of a very real problem. The scrap bin and waste tubs effectively act as predetermined receptacles of exceptions. But in the case of plastics manufacturing, no such physical evidence is available and the employees' lack of training remained an undetermined factor, for no matter how little they understood the operation of the front end of the machines, they knew only too well the efficacy of the grinder in removing evidence. The management of this particular plant instituted a simple plan, as spelled out in Chapter 2. Any time a plan was not going as scheduled, they asked the foremen to write out the reason why. In this way the lack of planning was identified in the second day of the documentation. By the third day the manager had set up a training session for his employees.

For years an unidentified factor had hampered the effective production of this plant. Yet in two days of documentation, the cycle of inefficiency had been broken, and a level of production, hitherto, unimagined by management had been attained. Once a seventy-man plant with a budget increase calling for an additional twenty-five to thirty employees to meet the required production, they are presently operating at the level of fifty-five to sixty employees and producing in excess of their budget forecast. Why? Quite simply because they now document their exceptions at the same time they are taking action to correct them. Errors and mistakes are identified immediately and are no longer reworked into the new plans. This operation saved the cost of twenty-five to thirty employees working 48 hours each week for a year at a cost of $4 plus per hour or somewhere in the neighborhood of $250,000 to $300,000 annually.

CERTIFYING THE FACTS

A salesman's expense sheet is a convenient means of considering the importance of certifying facts in a Management by Exception system. If a commission salesman is on a draw to "cover expenses—up to $200 per week," precious few, if any, such salesmen ever have expenses less than that sum unless, of course, there is some attempt to ascertain the facts of the expenses themselves. A situation of this sort should be easy enough to follow and control, but such is rarely the case. In the larger sales forces the expenses invariably go to the accounting department for approval. Accountants, for all their many virtues, are trained to add columns of figures; they are *not* trained to evaluate the validity of expenses. Some managements will supply their accounting staffs with guidelines in the form of "aids," but most of them have no method of determining the validity of the expenses.

A SIMPLE CASE IN POINT

At one time a brewing company allowed its entire sales force to send their expense vouchers directly to the accounting department. The form used was a weekly accounting sheet utterly devoid of any sales information. When a new system of managing this sales force by exception was designed, the expense voucher was added to the call report as a line entry. For the first time the regional and division sales managers were able to scan the results of the sales efforts *and* their costs at a single glance. They were, thus, enabled to certify the validity of the figures at the same time they evaluated their sales plans. Needless to add, the sales expenses dropped off dramatically; about $50 per week per salesman. This reduction amounted to $457,600 less salesmen's expenses. In the same year, this company increased sales.

A METHOD FOR CERTIFYING FACTS

Salesmen are not the only employees who will do a better job if their actions can be certified. Eventually the simple listing of exceptions will deteriorate if there is no sound method of verifying the certainty of the facts. One method of determining if the exceptions are realistic is to equate them to volume, pieces, parts, cases or time. Equation of this sort allows management to add up the exceptions as well as the accepted production figures and determine if the totals are within the capacities of the equipment. This method is best applied when the nature of the work is uniform, and there is little change in the mix. The industrial towel case, cited earlier, is a good example of what may be done when the mix is stable. Here, all variances could be and were spelled out in the loss of folded towel production. The plan was based on the belief that each employee was capable of a given output. The supervisor then issued a set number of cards each hour in accordance with the employee's established performance. Each bundle had a card attached. Upon completion of each hour the supervisor counted the remaining cards and made the appropriate notation on his exception report (see Figure 10) citing the reasons for lost production. This procedure not only allowed management to know just what the problems were but also, by certifying the facts, to determine how much improvement might be made when a reason for lost production was resolved.

This method of exception fact certification has become a very useful tool in plants where the new managers want modern equipment, and the older hands feel that such expenditure is not justifiable. In the case of the industrial towels, the action and documentation were initially used to determine how much production was lost due to lack of material available (you remember the plaint: "Those morons ran out of work . . ."). The management of the industrial laundry was quick to identify the real cost of the heretofore cost saving approach of keeping the towel inventory low to avoid the buildup of a capital investment. But in light of the lost production of the towel department, this proved to be a false economy. After determining the problem and weighing its cost, all of the towel folders were sent home for a day *with* pay. With this one day lag a towel supply was built up between the drying tumblers and the folding operation. Thus, when the folders returned the following day, they had their most perplexing problem solved by management through the simple use of the action documentation, twins of a Management by Exception System. The certification of the facts through this method allowed management to discover that their previously unchallenged opinion on the cost of inventory buildup had crumbled under the weight of action certification.

Exception Report

AREA: SHIFT: DATE:

Time Period	*Reason*	*Corrective Action Taken*	*Cause Code*

CAUSES OF LOST PRODUCTION

A. Off Scheduled Delivery
B. Mechanical Breakdown
C. Training Required
D. Security Interruption
E. Weather
F. Site Condition Change
G. Equipment Shortage
H. Merchandise Not Available
I. Haul Backs
J. Unloading Delay
K. Insufficient Truck Capacity

FIGURE 10

TWO BEFORE AND AFTER CASES:

A. The shelf talkers

A California supermarket grocery chain had four markets in Nevada. The back rooms of each of these stores were jammed with inventory, and a detailed check of the items in supply revealed that in almost every case, they were the same as those items stocked on the shelves. This situation posed a most puzzling problem to the company's management, since it was not the case in any of their other stores. Not only were they overinventoried on stocked items, they were running as high as 30% out of stock conditions in these same stores. The problem was unraveled by the internal systems group through a documentation of the movement of some of the key in and out items. Once documented, the reason for the shortages and overages was apparent—a lack of what is known in the grocery industry as "in house shelf talkers." These are nothing more than tags placed as unobtrusively as possible on the shelves to indicate to the individual ordering the replacement stock what should be there and how much more should be ordered. Throughout the rest of the chain, these shelf talkers were part of the ordering system; in Nevada, however, the local field superintendent felt that their cost could not be justified. Consequently, the grocery clerks assigned the task of making up the shipment orders would make their decisions by first observing the vacancy in a shelf, then looking to the left or right to determine what was missing. All of which was fine—for a time. But when an item went out of stock completely, the clerk would order the remaining product which was the slower mover. From there it was only a matter of time until the back room was clogged with the items that didn't move. Once the systems people identified the problem, the shelf talkers were up and on the shelves in a week. The inventory in the back rooms shrank and the consumer, the luckless victim of actions taken without documenting the facts, now had his favorite selections available once more. Happier still was the management, for the mysterious loss of business in the markets was effectively reversed.

This group of stores soon were reflecting greater sales and an increased profit. By the end of six months the four stores were operating at the highest dollars per man hour in the chain. The profit increase totaled over $112,000 by the end of the first year. Labor was being applied, by management, in the right direction.

This was a case of a more far reaching example of Management by Exception, than merely a failure to document the facts. First and always, the plan must be firmly in place before any attempt is made to document exceptions. The shelf talkers were themselves a plan. Their absence made it necessary to track the movement of certain key items and the total relationship of products was obscure. The field superintendent's false economy was responsible for serious losses, and this is doubly interesting, in view of the fact that opponents of Management by Exception Systems will inevitably complain about the costs of planning and documentation. It is, therefore, extremely important for the implementor of any exception system to know what some of the real costs are before he attempts to effect any changes.

B. The missing paper rolls

The Flexible Packaging Division of a major paper producing company was experiencing serious production delays due to the irregularities of their raw paper stock. The problem was that the Flexible Packaging Division's paper rolls came from their own company mills. Any effort to pinpoint production losses was, not surprisingly, frowned upon and considered excuse-making on the part of the division. When a uniform system of production planning was married to an exception reporting system with documentation of the facts, the complaining was transformed into cold statistical evidence. A method of charge backs was effected and the quality of the raw paper rolls improved, as well as the compensation for loss when it occurred. The profitability of the one division was now more accurately reflected and many of the problems eliminated.

MALFUNCTIONING UTILITIES

In discussing changes effected once the facts are known, it should be noted that many plants are adversely affected by the malfunctioning of a certain utility. Because in so many plants almost no records are kept, there is never a compensation made when "the lights go out." A power failure in a production plant may cost many thousands of dollars. During data transmission on computers, a power failure can result in the loss of critical data. A malfunctioning telephone system may cost a company an order or give its customer service a questionable reputation. Still, management seldom documents such facts in order to determine the loss and bill the party responsible.

With the advent of that new wonder of modern office equipment, the copying machine, we have the most common day to day loss going undocumented and costing the consumer millions of dollars. Few companies maintain tight controls on their reproducing machines and yet, regardless of the manufacturer, those machines are plagued by recurrent malfunctioning. In one regional market, a major copying corporation maintains a repair maintenance staff equal to one repair hour for every twenty hours of equipment. This statistic in itself is proof of the necessity of documenting the fact of equipment malfunction. The standard practice of these service men is to "credit" the consumer with X number of copies for the malfunctioning equipment. Not infrequently, the serviceman will "credit" the office manager with a hundred copies more than he actually had. But had that same happy office manager maintained a simple method of documenting the exceptions on a routine basis, he might have been "credited" with his cost of the paper, the toner (which is, by the way, more expensive than often realized), the lost labor, lost equipment time and percentage loss of that element he will have to replace when the thirty thousand copies have been run—good or bad. This is not to mention any determination of the validity of the copies run in the first place and their authorization, that is, the plan.

Figures 11 and 11a show a simple method of documenting the facts. With any variation from this theme, it will be necessary for the system designer or manager to determine the costs of a given operation. This same form will work successfully in telephone logs, delivery trips, receiving reports and any similar procedures. It would be foolhardy to advocate a tally on every aspect of business life, but in cases where several departments and individuals use the same equipment or services, someone should be documenting the facts of that use. The assumption is that when the facts are known, positive changes can be effected.

Copier Log

Date	*Meter Reading*	*Project Number*	*What Copied*	*Number of Originals*	*Number of Copies per Original*	*By Whom*

FIGURE 11

Wat Line Record

WEEK ENDING

Call Date	O U T	I N	*Time Begin Time End*	*Project or Company Number*	*To Whom*	*From Whom*	*Time Elapsed*

FIGURE 11A

IDEAS FOR IMPLEMENTATION

Regardless of the level of management concerned with action and documentation, the implementation of even the simplest form will be difficult unless one begins with a fundamental plan. Consider again the example of the telephone or copier log. By itself, a complex or laborious employee tally will do little more than irritate the habitual users of the equipment. Before implementing the log, one should be aware of the flow problems and should have some clear picture of what he expects to attain through the log. Once these facts have been established, the designer should also take the time to walk the flow through himself, fill out a complete sheet, carry it to its final resting place and there complete it. Oftentimes, forms are implemented because they were successful in another operation or another area. No effort is made to tailor the form to the current situation or to implement it with a thorough knowledge of the eventual participants. The following are simple rules to observe in the implementation of a documentation system:

1. Determine the purpose of the form.
2. Know the "ball park" answers to the items recorded.
3. Have a method of certifying the facts.
4. Predetermine the necessary information blanks.

5. Give your method of documentation a dress rehearsal prior to implementation; that is, de-bug it *before* it goes into use.
6. Don't attempt to implement the form outside the normal chain of command.
7. Follow up on the form during its infancy; be certain it is being used properly.
8. Make provisions for the ultimate disposition of the form.
9. Determine the duration of the form prior to implementation—is it a temporary, permanent or transition form?

These rules are good ones to follow in the implementation of any systems form, but they are especially helpful in the development type forms mentioned in this chapter. In establishing the methods of identifying the actions and documenting them, one must always remember that the purpose is to effect a better plan through the prudent use of heretofore unknown information on reasons for exceptions to that plan. In later chapters specific examples of a fully integrated exception system will be shown; the forms we have considered here are only for the primary or initial aspect of an exception system. They are much like the ABC's of grade school and must be mastered before one can hope to move into the more complex areas of standard costing, economic order quantity, and other methods of manpower, material and money controls.

MANAGEMENT BY EXCEPTION POINTERS

1. It is vital to provide a method for recording exceptions at the execution point of any plan.
2. Accurate exception recording will iron out flaws in a plan and make for effective revisions of that plan.
3. Without all of the essential facts acquired through documentation, any revisions of the original plan are likely to be inadequate.
4. All exceptions to the plan should be documented immediately upon their discovery.
5. You must be prepared to certify the facts and figures that occur in all documentation by exception. Such certification may also be a means of determining the validity of expenses.
6. By equating exceptions to volume, pieces, parts, cases or time, you can often determine how realistic exceptions are.
7. Follow the nine simple rules for implementing a documentation system suggested at the end of this chapter.

4

PREDETERMINING EXCEPTIONS THROUGH IDENTIFICATION AND CLASSIFICATION

COMMON MISTAKES IN ESTABLISHING MANAGEMENT BY EXCEPTION MECHANICS

In almost all cases in which a good planning system has been established and tied closely to a reporting system, there still exists the glaring absence of a method for collecting and using exceptions that inevitably arise between the initial plan and the final report. Because of this void, many otherwise good systems fail to serve the people using them, and their operations flounder. The first of the many possible weaknesses one is apt to discover in the mechanics of any system is its inability to pinpoint why the plan was not executed as originally designed. Ordinarily, this particular void occurs because the author of the system did not know what problems existed or were likely to exist in the first place. Of course, one must assume that the basic essentials of an exception system, as covered in Chapters One through Three, are indeed in operation. But even if the system's author was aware of the several exceptions that might occur, it is likely that he did not share his knowledge with those using the system through the use of preprinted spaces on the reporting forms. Thus, the most common error in a system of Management by Exception is often the inability to identify the exception itself.

In addition, when the exception is identified and documented, it is not infrequent for the system to fail to provide broad classifications for the exceptions themselves.

A major copper producing firm is most proud of its "top ten" report. This report lists the ten most important exceptions in their production units for the past month. While the intention is good, the results are not as significant as they could be. Each month all the production management re-invents the wheel, so to speak, and no basic categories are ever established by the top management. Therefore, month after month, this firm compares apples to oranges always expressing it in a different manner. While the energy is there, the results are not.

PROBLEMS THAT DO NOT SURFACE

In systems in which this lack of exception classifications is found, another mistake almost certainly will follow, and that is the use of an improper unit of measure for identifying and recording. In a large Hawaiian maintenance operation attempting to implement a Management by Exception System, it was noted that exceptions were recorded in the loss of man-minutes, with no predetermined classification provided for that entry on the reporting form. Needless to say, the manager of that particular sugar plantation was faced each week with a statement of the hundreds of man-hours lost in his operation. In this case the manager now knew, by exception to his supervisor's plans, the supposed exact amount of time his operations cost him. However, he really didn't know a great deal more than he had before the system was established. In fact, he was merely reminded of the magnitude of his loss. The mechanics of the system were operative, but the real problems were not surfacing.

Everyday life provides numerous other examples of systems in which problems are not surfacing. Consider for a moment the customer service in a bank, an airline ticket counter or a supermarket checkout line. In each of these situations, one inevitably finds a log jam of backed up lines. Why? Simply because management does not know just why the lines occur. And week after endless week no effort is made to ease the irritation of the consumer, because the managers of these operations have no means of discovering the reasons for the cumbersome, lengthy lines. Even if they initiated a plan to handle the volume (and few do), they would not know what caused the plan to go awry. The reason is that their systems lack an adequate soothing and causing coding device. Ask the next person serving you in a long and tedious line why it occurs, and what they are doing about it. Sadly, they almost certainly will not have the answers.

PRE-PLANNING BASED ON OBSERVABLE FACTS

In establishing a system in which the unknown is a significant factor, it is obviously essential for the known to be identified and provided for well in advance. In our examples cited above, the managers of those operations could tell you that there are certain common denominators responsible for the interminable lines, which is to say there are exceptions to the overall exceptions themselves. In customer service jam-ups the reason for the problem is almost always the same: all the people in the line are not in need of equal service. Prior to establishing the plan for a particular aisle, the manager should predetermine an average time/service ratio for each customer, have the clerk record exceptions that exceed that ratio and make educated guesses for the reasons for such exceptions. The clerk could then, in effect, sort the wheat from the chaff, and the manager could know at the end of a single day which problems were contributing to his backed-up lines.

As an example, let us compare the time required to ticket the little old lady from Pasadena who wants to go round the world on Ozark Airlines (the exception), as opposed to the commercial traveler with an airline credit card who wants a one-way flight on United Airlines flight 236 from Denver to Chicago (the routine). Because the passenger agent serves the exception, irate businessmen build up the line behind the little old lady.

Now, the management problems encountered in the lengthy supermarket lines and those at the sugar plantation are essentially the same. They both reflect the failure of management to single out the problem through the use of their system. In the case of the sugar plantation, this failure spells the loss of productivity through the needless use of excess man-hours. In the case of the customer service operations, it spells an ultimate loss of business through bad service. Yet, in both cases the root of the problem is the same: the lack of a predetermined category for the documentation of the exceptions.

If, upon implementation of a planning and reporting system, you make provision for documenting exceptions to the plans, you have taken the first concrete step toward establishing a system of Management by Exception. In these predetermined categories lie the solutions to the problems that prevent the smooth execution of the plan. No airline president, supermarket manager or banker wants to have bad customer service, and most have done the best they can to avoid it. But the failure to provide the clerk at the operations level with a simple tallying device has resulted in just the opposite of the fond expectations. It should be clear, then, that if you are to establish a system of problem identification, the very lowest operations level must have a predetermined method of placing the exceptions in appropriate categories. An example of such a method is found in Figure 9. This form may be used in almost any operation, and if it is properly recapped and carried up the chain of command, it may well be the only basic tool needed for the continual upgrading of the system. Naturally, predetermination of problems will change as management takes action on those initial problems.

PREDETERMINING WHICH PROBLEMS WILL EXIST

While some problems are universal, many are unique to a given industry. But universal or not, management must always determine how they bear on its particular operation. Because this is so, it is necessary for each manager to identify the major problems in his area of responsibility. Universal problems are often classified under the broad category of "lack of. . . ". Some notable examples are lack of training, tools, materials, instructions or equipment. The unique problems are ordinarily more specialized, as in the examples of the customer services operations. In those cases nothing is lacking; quite the contrary, an overabundance exists which has not been adequately prepared for; such as for the airline: needed reservations, altered reservations, credit checks, incorrect flight information, return reservations and a host of other contingencies. The reason such exceptions are listed here is that, once cited, just about everyone has an opinion on what the problems might be. And there is the key. If the right people set the predetermined categories, then those with less experience will be guided into pointing out solutions through compiling numerical analyses of the problems. After all, if everyone could tell a manager which problems caused his plan to go off course, then he could easily compose a better plan the next time. The difficulty is that there are simply not enough hours in a day for a manager to listen to all of the problems. The method of identifying the exception and placing it in a predetermined category will allow the manager to gain perspective on the failure of his plan.

As an adjunct to the exception tool cited in Figure 9, we can now add the predetermined reasons for the failure of the plan to operate in predictable fashion. Consider again the airline ticket counter jam and apply this device to the individual clerks at their counters. On completion of a day, the manager would know why the lines existed and what should be done to alleviate the situation. To pursue the example further, suppose the category that emerged most frequently was labeled "Did not have reservations." Clearly, the manager could take the proper steps the following day to eliminate this problem. This sort of Management by Exception goes on constantly. The supermarket check out aisle for those shoppers with under six items is another example of extraction of exceptions to provide speedier service. The airlines have made an effort to employ this technique through the use of stewardess-type assistants approaching customers with offers of help. Unfortunately, however, they have not as yet learned how to screen customers and direct them to the specialized ticket clerks, so at best they only level the number of people behind each line.

FAILURE TO DETERMINE PROBLEMS COMMON TO NEW OPERATIONS

Most managers have to undergo a plant or operations move only once in their business lives, and most are profoundly grateful. In such moves we find a woeful lack of Management by Exception. An electronics firm in Los Angeles moved from six different smaller locations into a magnificent new plant. The management of that company spent the first two months at its new site looking for the various departments and employees. The mail room girl broke down in tears the first day, because she couldn't find the president's office. Customer service became a nightmare and inventory control a shambles. Odd as it might seem, this is not an isolated example. Many managements shudder at the thought of a plant move or a new market grand opening. Why? Curiously, they seem to abandon all of their knowledge about systems of Management by Exception and approach the problem as though it were unique to them. Yet, by applying the simple exception-to-the-plan technique to any move, one will discover that, once the known is established, a predetermination of the exceptions will fall easily into place.

CASE IN POINT

A major supermarket chain in Pennsylvania lost a quarter of a million dollars when it opened a new operation in New Jersey. The management had contracted for the opening of twelve more operations over a three year period, and they were understandably panicky at the loss of their first venture. A review of the reasons for the loss revealed that no detailed plan had ever been established in the first place. By the time the second move was made, such a plan did exist, and included in the reporting system was a place for predetermined exceptions. As a consequence, the loss diminished to $65,000 in the same time period. By continuing to apply this knowledge and by taking action on exceptions, this management will have its third store opening at a break even point.

THE START-UP SYNDROME

How many times do shareholders, finding their dividends down, discover a clause in the president's report explaining that the start-up costs of a plant had run higher than expected? What this clause really says is that the president and his team haven't been using the basics of Management by Exception. The present chapter could be entitled "Separating the Wheat from the Chaff." The ability to anticipate problems is as vital as the ability to solve them. It is an unfortunate fact that the usual plant start-up fails to employ even a single element of the Management by Exception technique. Here again, the plan and report are essential to any business endeavor, but the plan will only succeed if the exception is identified, categorized and acted upon before the plan is revised and the exception problems eliminated.

CASE IN POINT

A company in the water heater, air conditioning and gas stove business spent over half a million dollars installing a Management by Exception system in its several operations. The system worked with considerable success. As the business grew, it was determined that the older physical plants would be inadequate for future needs and that many of the operations could be profitably combined in a new location. Six years earlier, they had made a similar move and it had been disasterous to their customer service, so they were understandably apprehensive over the coming relocation. This time, however, they profited from their experience. Before proceeding too far, they called in the implementors of their system and obtained help in applying the same rules to the move that had been applied in their current production. The rules were, in fact, the plan, and the second move went smoothly and profits soared. What had been a disaster before was now a perfectly controlled operation. This company had learned the hard way that many unanticipated problems were bound to arise. When problems did arise, they were grouped into categories and dealt with properly and expediently. The move was accomplished on schedule, even though there were as many problems as before; the difference was that this time the management was prepared for them.

PROVIDING GENERAL CATEGORIES: A CASE IN POINT

Let us turn once more to our example of the sugar plantation manager in Hawaii. In that instance the absence of categories for separating lost time in the operation left the manager with scarcely any more knowledge than he had at the outset. The ultimate solution to this type of problem will reflect what can be achieved through the addition of the proper predetermined categories.

This manager decided he could no longer accept the total figure each week, as it simply told him what he already knew: his plans were badly off schedule. He determined it would be necessary to get the required information in working condition so that proper action could be taken and better plans prepared. To this end, he instructed his superintendents to list all the reasons they knew for the plan's failure. Next, he took the list (which included over fifty different reasons) and singled out the major nine, relegating all of the others to a tenth category. He then had all of his line supervision place all the time lost into one of the ten categories. At the end of the first week, he knew which problem was his greatest, and he directed all of his attention toward correcting this problem. Whereas before, he had relied on his wits and luck to determine solutions for the lost time, now he knew which category was in fact responsible for the major portion of the loss. As it happened, the category was labelled "lack of skill," so he set up training classes and hired instructors. With the upgrading of his personnel, this category fell from the top of the list and he was able to set about the next categories in turn. The solution, then, for one problem or category of problems is best determined by first identifying exceptions to the plan, as it is such exceptions that cause the plan to consume more manpower or materials than originally predicted.

A METHOD OF SORTING OUT POTENTIAL PROBLEMS

It is obvious that Management by Exception functions most successfully when old problems are solved. Such solution allows heretofore hidden problems to appear. The plantation manager arbitrarily grouped the exceptions into ten categories and directed his attention toward a solution of the one consuming the largest amount of time. From this start he was working toward the day when the tenth category of miscellaneous problems would be the largest and the last. But when he arrives at category ten, he is back on the horns of the same dilemma. Why? Because this is true, it becomes necessary as the improvement of the system of Management by Exception proceeds to introduce a new element in order to bring to the surface unknown or secondary problems. To do so, an alert systems man will add a new dimension to the form in Figure 9. Now the line supervisor will be allowed to place the reason and action taken on the exception report itself, though, of course, management must always place the exceptions in categories for easy communication up the chain of command. But, at the line level the supervisor must have the power to help flush out new problems within the confines of the established categories. This procedure sets the stage for the various levels of Management by Exception reporting. It also documents the details of the exceptions and provides a mechanism for the identification of otherwise unknown categories, (see Figure 10). By adding the reason and the action taken, and by cross coding these into categories, management now has available the information needed to add new categories while discarding old or solved ones.

Medical advances in the past three decades provide an excellent example of an entire profession identifying exceptions and resolving them, only to be confronted with new problems previously classified as minor. At the turn of the century, tuberculosis was a dreadful killer. Later, polio appeared to take its place. Today, leukemia, all but unknown seventy years ago, ranks as a major disease. The constant re-direction of medical effort is, in broad terms, an apt example of the application of the Management by Exception system.

TWO CASES OF SORTING PROBLEMS IN ADVANCE

A. The medical laboratory

A medical laboratory owned and established by a group of doctors persisted in showing a steady decline in profits. By the middle of its fifth year, this laboratory was facing bankruptcy. Upon examination, the conditions found were those that usually prevail when management fails to separate the wheat from the chaff in its operation. In this case no manager, shareholder or board member had the same opinion regarding the reasons for the laboratory's failure. Quite the contrary, each individual had a distinct idea for the solution of the problems at hand. The operation was at the mercy, for the most part, of groundless opinion and prejudice on the part of every person associated with it. Marketing experts had been hired and fired. Systems experts, personnel experts, medical experts had all been consulted with the same results.

As conditions rapidly worsened, the board made the decision to hire some experts in the field of management, who initiated a Management by Exception system the first week. All users of the laboratory's services were polled and asked why they used the laboratory and what were the problems. These problems were quickly formalized into categories, and a planning/reporting system was established with an exception reporting mechanism built in. Within one month the threat of bankruptcy was removed, and the laboratory was on the way to improved customer service as well as an expanded volume of tests.

The first year following these improvements this small laboratory was operating at a $25,000 net profit with no increase in the test costs to the doctor owners. The board of directors was placed in a position of managing the affairs of the operation by exception to their approved plan. Prior to the implementation of this system, they had no method of sorting out the problems, let alone knowing which were valid and which demanded immediate solution. Had this laboratory continued on its original course, it would surely be out of business today.

B. The manufacturing company

Consider another example. A manufacturing company in central Illinois was plagued by its inability to meet sales requirements during the winter months. They had always believed that they lacked sufficient capacity for manufacturing their requirements when the peak load hit. For years they had accumulated a large stock of their product and spent considerable amount of money warehousing the summer production. Thus, when they hit a bottleneck, everyone worked feverishly to solve the problem. As commendable as this "will-do" attitude on the part of the employees was, it was a poor substitute for the identification of the problems they so willingly—and laboriously—worked themselves out of. And, as the economic picture changed and labor increased the price of production, the company was sold to a conglomerate. The executives of that organization relied far less on employee good will and much more on managing their interests by exception. They called the head of the Illinois company into their main office and explained the new method of operation. This method was nothing other than managing the operation by exception, which meant that first the exceptions would have to be categorized and analyzed to determine just what the real problems were. After this was accomplished, the company was able to close out several of its summer production warehouses within the span of a single year. The management had found that its production was increasing in capacity as more and more previously unidentified problems were solved. The elimination of these problems increased the company's capacity to such an extent that winter rushes became a thing of the past, and the company eventually emerged as the largest single profit center for the conglomerate.

This conglomerate was into advanced technological manufacturing, producing such items as laser beams, automatic aircraft landing devices, electronics and power equipment. Their plants stretched over all the United States and overseas. It was no easy task for the space heater company in Illinois to show the largest profit in that kind of company. Yet it did, with a $2,000,000 profit, one year after Managing by Exception.

SOME FORMS FOR DISCOVERING HIDDEN CAUSES OF PLANS NOT EXECUTED

The forms used to illustrate methods of focusing on problems indentified through Management by Exception systems (Figures 9 and 10) have many and varied applications in a number of industries. While the basics are the same, the applications may vary from one industry to the next. Refer again to the sugar plantation manager's problems. In his particular application of Management by Exception, it was noted that the reported item was man-hours lost. The selection of that unit of measure was unfortunate, as the growth of that industry was based on large numbers of unskilled labor. Many of the plantation workers and even some of the foremen were unable to speak English and lacked any formal education. To attempt to equate work with standard hours of production was clearly not the solution to the problem. The simple fact is that regardless of the industry, the decision on how detailed exception reporting should be, must be made in accordance with the circumstances of the operation. There is, unfortunately, no magic formula. In the plantation case the elimination of the man-minutes and man-hours ratio proved to be not only a welcome relief for the line foremen, who were hard pressed to understand it in the first place, but also the revised form of exception reporting came to be more meaningful to the plantation manager as well. The end result was that the cumulation of incidents on a stroke tally basis was sufficient to make a useful report and allowed all concerned to concentrate on elimination of the problem, rather than its documentation.

A clerical operation lends itself to precision more than most and, yet, is often handled far more loosely than, say a foundry. In a foundry, time and equipment work in distinct relationship to each other. The overhead crane, time in the molds, cooling time—all are significant. In almost all clerical operations the precision of time is measured in half days at best. Since this is true, one must remember that in setting up a Management by Exception System for a clerical operation, there is likely to be much more chaff than wheat. As a matter of fact, most such operations are wasteful simply because the manager cannot tell the difference between essential work and work which can wait. An exception reporting system can be locked into the flow controls, which will allow for the application of the same technique described for the sugar plantation. In clerical operations a listing of all the work to be accomplished and a match-up of the volume and time requirements to this list will ordinarily indicate that all the work load for a department and for the individual employee lends itself to the ten category approach. Once this is accomplished, the manager of the operation will have regained control of his department through exception reporting. And if the items in the tenth category reflect an increase beyond the first nine, then the detail of the individual report will come to the attention of management for review and rearrangement. An example of the method of identifying clerical workloads and managing the typical clerical operation by exception is illustrated in Figure 12.

Clerical Flow Report

DATE
EMPLOYEE

ACTIVITIES	Unit of	*Monday*		*Tuesday*		*Wednesday*		*Thursday*		*Friday*		*Saturday*	
	Measure		C/O		C/O		C/O		C/O		C/O		C/O

FIGURE 12

Salesmen and sales forces have long been burdened by laborious reporting systems. All of these reports notwithstanding, precious few sales managers clearly detail what they expect from their staff beyond moving the product, and almost none of them know the sales productivity of their men. Here, as in the clerical operation, detailing of time is not the element that will lead to a solution of the problem. A stroke tally or an incident notation is usually sufficient, if the categories are predetermined, to aid the manager in controlling his sales force by exception.

Figure 13 illustrates one sample of a national sales force's forms used first by the district managers to determine why a plan is not executed and what reasons are noted. In turn, the regional managers add their exceptions to the reports and forward them to the division vice presidents, who do the same, and the forms ultimately arrive in the office of the general manager of sales for the company. A major brewery in the Midwest made some amazing discoveries when it implemented this system of Management by Exception. Several salesmen no longer sell for that brewery, but sales moved from −5% to +12% in the first six months of this system's implementation.

This change in market position was equally reflected in the profit from loss statements issued by this company. From a monthly loss of over $21,000 they

Exception Report

FROM
DATE

Exception	*Reason*	*Cause Code*

Cause Code

A. Buyer Out
B. Approved Change
C. Car Trouble
D. Rotation or Service Problem
E. Special Pricing by Competitor
F. Sickness

FIGURE 13

rose to $50,000 profit. By the end of the first year they had turned an annual $250,000 loss into a $600,000 gain, a change of $850,000 in a single year. Salesmen are so glib they can charm the very birds from the trees, and if one has to manage a national force of such charmers, he had better have some tool for separating the wheat from the chaff. The first major category for this particular company was, astonishingly, auto breakdown. This category was established by a stroke tally of incident in the first month of implementation of the system, and it seemed especially odd in view of the fact that the company furnished the cars and paid for their repair. Yet there it was : ''automotive problems'' were impeding the proper execution of the plan. Need I add, that auto repair no longer proves to be the principal reason for lagging beer sales?

Service operations have been mentioned before in this chapter, and they provide the occasion for the most dramatically effective results of Management by Exception. While other industries are largely concealed from public view, the neighborhood supermarket enjoys no such anonymity. Here, the man on the street can witness first hand the failures of Management by Exception on an hourly basis. Because very few managers in this industry make an adequate plan for their operation, Management by Exception is almost impossible. If you doubt that statement, ask yourself when you last saw the manager of a grocery store bagging groceries himself. Yesterday? More than likely. Some few enlightened supermarket chains have instituted a Management by Exception policy, and they follow the plan and thus, are able to sift the wheat from the chaff. In the case of the

Store Supervisors Check Sheet

Store Number

Period	*Condition*	*Assigned to*	*Code*

FIGURE 14

supermarket, the stroke tally is not meaningful enough because, while the time element is important, the exceptions related to so many man hours are not. A simple check sheet made every hour and cross coded to predetermined categories will point the way to not only better customer service but to the smoother execution of future plans as well. Figure 14 illustrates a simple check sheet which, linked with an hourly walk through the store by the manager, will tell him where the exceptions are arising. These exceptions can then be directed up the chain of command until the president knows precisely what is the greatest single problem in his entire operation. And knowing that problem will pave the way for smoother operation.

MANAGEMENT BY EXCEPTION POINTERS

1. The most common flaw in a system of Management by Exception is the inability to identify the exception itself.
2. Once the exceptions are identified, it is necessary to group them in broad categories or classifications.
3. The systems man must encourage each manager to identify the major problems in his area of responsibility.
4. Once all of the known factors are established, predetermination of exceptions will follow naturally.
5. Work from the category of most frequent exceptions to that of those least frequent.
6. The forms represented in Figures 9-14 will aid in discovering hidden causes of plans not executed.

5

ACTIVATING THE SYSTEM THAT SPOTLIGHTS THE BIGGEST PROBLEMS

WHAT IS THE BIGGEST SINGLE PROBLEM IN YOUR COMPANY TODAY?

Most managers are skilled at acting on problems once they have been identified. However, most of them, from the line supervisor to the chairman of the board, literally do not know what those problems are, let alone what the biggest single one may be. Ask a manager at any level to describe the major problem in his operation and more often than not, the response will be a quizzical look followed by some evasive jargon. Astonishing as it may seem, it is not unusual to find very large and apparently thriving concerns whose management is unable to identify precise problems of *any* magnitude, great or small. And, it is just this sort of inability that stifles growth and productivity.

IDENTIFYING THE BIGGEST PROBLEM

In an effort to identify the biggest problem, many managers will rely on information which may not be generated from within the immediate frameworks of their own systems. Unfortunately, such managers tend to be overly credulous of data originating outside their systems, even though they may have contrary information directly before them. Managers, being human, are influenced by their more vocal subordinates. Often an employee will blow a problem far out of proportion in order to serve his own needs or solidify a real or imagined vantage point, and a manager may find himself at the mercy of such an aggressive subordinate. An individual who complains loudly enough and often enough will frequently find his complaint carried to the very highest levels of command within a company, regardless of how insignificant his problem may be.

CASE IN POINT

In a very large Midwestern dairy the quality control inspector, a chemical engineer, persisted in maintaining that the bacteria count in the milk was dangerously high. He was so forceful in both his remarks and his reports that eventually the situation came to the attention of the company's president. This president proceeded to institute a massive sanitation program, until he realized that the alleged high bacteria count and the inspector's ambition for more subordinates, finally, for more power, were directly proportional. This realization came when the manager of internal systems brought to the president's attention comparative charts reflecting the bacteria count of his dairy, relative to all the other dairies in that local market. What those charts demonstrated was that his operation had a twenty-five percent lower bacteria count than the others and a consistently safe pattern of bacteria. Yet, before he saw this conclusive information, he had accepted as truth, what was in fact, the inspector's fanciful notion that the greatest single problem in the dairy was quality control of the sanitation.

This example, isolated and particular though it may be, illustrates how employees acting outside the frame of a system may maximize lesser problems and, for reasons of their own, even conjure up illusory problems which indeed do not exist at all. How then can a manager identify his greatest single problem? Clearly, such identification will come only through the use of a system which considers uniformly and on a routine basis all the major exceptions. These exceptions must be categorized and put into the form of a report. This report should tell at a glance what that problem is and document it with evidence from every supervisor operating within the system, accounting for every hour of every area of the operation.

WHY COMPANIES DO NOT KNOW THEIR MAJOR PROBLEMS

Most companies never discover their major problem simply because they lack the kind of system described above. Human frailties such as strong willed or self-serving employees, personnel conflicts, malingering and inter-office politics may get in the way, and the result may be chaos. Add to those that complex of difficulties any industry is heir to—growing backlogs, behind schedule situations, holidays, peak seasons, seasonal slumps—and the ultimate result could very well be disastrous. Regardless of all the various reasons advanced to explain why a company doesn't know its major problem, the *real* reason always comes down to the failure of the system to pinpoint and document that problem. Until this first step is taken, lesser problems will continue to proliferate, cloud the air, divert the manager into minutiae, that is not his province, and cost the company untold man hours and dollars.

TWO CASES IN POINT

An Ohio based company, supplying Ford Motor Company with the door frames used in passenger car manufacturing, discovered that it was scrapping twelve out of every fourteen frames produced in the plant. Its president used the typical means of identifying problems found in most industries today: he called in the heads of his various departments for an explanation of why so many frames were unsuitable for sale. The engineers told him that the problem lay in the new curvature window configuration used in this year's model car. In the past no such problem existed because the windows were flat, and all the jigs would match, whereas, in this year's model the windows curved not only from front to back but from top to bottom. Since it was their first encounter with this problem, the engineers felt it could be worked out with next year's model through better engineering technique. In the meantime, however, it would be extremely difficult to supply Ford this year, unless an immediate engineering change was forthcoming. The manufacturing manager confirmed much the same information but could not understand why the frames did not match. The jigs used to fit the pieces prior to cutting had been measured, re-measured, checked and double checked in order to prove that they were correct. The purchasing agent was asked if any specification in the steel had changed. His answer was negative, yet, the situation continued to persist. During the course of implementing a new exception system, one of the industrial engineers on the floor noticed that, while the various pieces for the doorframe were cut on a jig, once cut, the pieces were mixed in tote boxes and matched up at the welding station with no identification of left, right, top and bottom pieces. Ultimately, it was this mixing that proved to be the real problem; for, while the jig was used to cut the pieces, the same pieces cut together were not being welded together, and the scrapping of twelve out of fourteen frames was a direct result of the confusion of pieces in the tote bins, when they were assigned to the welding station. In this case, the company operated for quite a long time in ignorance of its major problem. As everyone had had his own opinion on the issue, no one had troubled to document the flow or use the information at hand to identify the problem as it occurred.

A West Coast printing company was losing money consistently. Its management believed the losses were caused by late delivery of plates coming from the lithography preparation department and by plates that were, for technical reasons, impossible to use. The losses were incurred over a span of two years, in spite of numerous attempts on the part of management to alleviate the situation. One solution was to replace the supervisor frequently. Another was to add more personnel and better equipment. Still, nothing seemed to work. Finally, management felt it necessary to document exactly how much the bad plates were costing. In executing this documentation other categories besides plate making were added to the presses themselves, in order to identify reasons for down time and the loss of profit. The first report was thought to be erroneous since it demostrated the plate making was not even a major factor in hours of down time for the presses. Rather, lack of volume emerged as the greatest single reason for the presses not operating steadily. Mechanical problems were the reason second in importance; the equipment was not functioning smoothly, regardless of the quality of the plates or the timeliness of their delivery. A third, significant reason for delay was customer alteration from the original specification. Lastly, ink trouble and a delay in paper delivery proved to be problems. The point is that management found for the first time—through a simple stroke tally every time the press went down—that what had originally been considered the major problem in the plant was, in fact, a relatively minor one. It was a problem, to be sure, but not one deserving that much of management's attention, until some of the others had been attended to. This particular instance led the company's management into a concerted effort in the sales field, rather than in the production plant itself. While the plates may have caused delays in production, the failure to have any production at all was at the root of more than half the idle machine hours. This is another example of a company that didn't know its major problems and, consequently, channelled management talent in the wrong direction. The reason? Absence of a plan, on the one hand, and the consequent presence of undocumented exceptions.

MISDIRECTED DRIVES

Many times management will commit the entire company to a drive for the elimination of what it conceives to be major operating problems. All too often, however, these drives are initiated with inadequate or partial information (as in the two cases cited previously), and result in little more than a futile, misguided expenditure of time and effort. Anyone who has been in business has doubtless been subjected to such drives, which frequently are dubbed by subordinates with such contemptuous titles as "The Corporation Paper Drive" or "The Accounting Miracle March." This sort of black humor arises from the employees' dim awareness of the misdirection of the drives; they seem to sense, however vaguely, that the wrong issues are under attack, while the real problems remain untouched.

TWO CASES IN POINT

Some years ago, a large scrap yard in the business of dismantling ships had some short interval scheduling systems people place a very effective short interval control over the day to day activities involved in ship dismantling. This system proved to be so successful that the company today has embarked on a major data processing automation program under the guidance of a nationally known accounting firm. Still, the comptroller will readily admit to a certain frustration on the part of management at the inability to pinpoint problems and take action on them. In an attempt to rectify this situation, the firm is spending upwards of half a million dollars to computerize the information being fed from a system six years old. Further, they have been obliged to employ an accounting firm to collect and automate this information. This is an excellent example of a false drive to eliminate a smaller problem; short interval schedule controls gave them a notable improvement over the former dismantling method, but were inadequate for pinpointing what had to be done in order to improve next. This inadequacy led the firm to believe that automation or, in effect, more of the same would somehow give them the information they currently did not possess. Once they finish automating the information, they will now have the only result possible, deeper frustration. They still do not know what the basic problems are, and where their efforts should be directed.

A data processing firm in Dallas, Texas, failed to show any profit after three years of operation, and the management felt very strongly that the reason for this failure was the inability to expand marketing activities. They called in a systems firm and directed them to increase those marketing activities immediately. The systems firm wisely refused, pointing out that the major problem had nothing to do with marketing at all, but rather with basic, ineffective methods of operating with the work currently in hand. An expanded marketing program would merely have compounded losses, since those losses were currently in direct proportion to the business they had already obtained. Because the internal system that was under attack failed to inform the local manager of his major problem, he disagreed vociferously with the systems people, dismissed them summarily, directed his entire energies into a marketing expansion and promptly went bankrupt six months later.

MANPOWER REDUCTION AS A SOLUTION FOR BAD MARKETING

Many firms are required to face annual layoffs because of an inability to market on a consistent basis. Manpower reduction, as a substitute for good marketing, is another example of a false drive that eliminates the smaller problem and leaves the larger ones untouched. In this case the smaller problem happens to be an excess of labor, caused by the inability of management to secure more volume input. Management operates in the dark because they have no mechanism to tell them why they are failing to sell their product or expand their market. Earlier, we discussed the case of the Midwestern beer company which used an exception tally to pinpoint its largest single problem, automobile breakdown. This same technique can be applied directly to types of accounts and how often they are called upon. In so doing, it is possible to pinpoint the failure of the sales force to market where the business is. Manpower reduction or plant shutdowns are often caused by the failure of management to direct the sales force into productive areas, and the result resembles the chicken/egg riddle. The plant shuts down because it doesn't have the business, and it doesn't have the business because the plant shut down. Finally, the plant is reduced to operating on a seasonal shut down basis. Once again, the reason can be traced to the failure of management to use exception information.

The same beer company mentioned previously categorized its accounts and quickly learned that during the winter months northern Wisconsin and Minnesota, heavy summer beer drinking areas, were using the same number of sales days to sell to the few tavern owners that remained active during that slack time. The situation was remedied when management laid out a specific plan detailing the number of sales days to be alloted against certain categories of accounts. When this was done by exception, areas of seasonal business were identified and the sales work days placed in more productive areas. The normal seasonal shut down was then not required, because the sales force was marketing where the business was. This was accomplished by the preparation of a plan aimed specifically at marketing information, rather than an overall geographical plan which kept people in place and accepted seasonal shut downs as a way of life.

Manpower reduction as a solution for bad marketing occurs far more frequently than is commonly known. With the exception of the food canning industry and holiday manufacturing firms, very few companies need be seasonal or cope with seasonal shut downs. Because this is true, manpower reduction can and should be looked upon as a large bit of exception information. Once management adopts this stance, it can begin ferreting out the real problems. Almost invariably, this will lead to pinpointing which marketing areas are lagging and when; then the proper steps can be taken to even the production itself. One company that followed this procedure pinpointed the inability of its sales force to sell a seasonal piece of equipment because the demand was gone, so they added a new product line to their plant. This company happened to manfacture heaters, and, when it added garden and lawn equipment to the production line, summer voids were filled. By identifying an apparent necessity for manpower reduction, the management established the need for a second product line.

FORCING THE PROBLEM TO THE SURFACE

If you were to manage a grocery store for the first time with no particular knowledge of the business, it is quite likely that you would be a better candidate to force the problems of the operation to the surface than a person who had spent several years in the grocery industry. The reason for this is that you would approach all problems as those to be identified and those to be solved. Figure 14 shows a typical store supervisor's check sheet. This sheet of paper can be employed successfully as a very basic means of identifying problems and forcing them to the surface. To employ it effectively, it is necessary for the supervisor of a store to make a periodic walk through his entire operation, perhaps at intervals as frequent as every two hours. During the course of these walks, everything he encounters that is wrong is noted on the sheet. On his first tour through the store, he writes up those which are, in his opinion, major problems. By so doing, he cites the largest problems first and saves the smaller ones for his next walk. In the interim he can assign work to part time employees or those completing a task at one end of the store or another. During his second walk he may find, to his surprise, that a problem identified in one end of the store has now recurred in another. The problem may take a variety of forms such as a spilled product, out of stock conditions, dirty shelves, broken displays, jam-ups at the check-out counters, etc. The nature of the problem is not particularly important at this time; what is vital is that it be systematically and routinely identified. By continuing this process during the course of the first day, a supervisor has documented evidence of what appeared to be the problems in his store, as they were identified every two hours. If it is continued throughout the week, he has, for the first time in a uniform method, a documentation of all the problems he was able to identify during that period. Now, at this point nothing has been done regarding the coding, classifying, grouping and solving of the problems; they have merely been identified. At week's end the supervisor should sit down and categorize or code those problems. Let us suppose, for example, that twelve times during the week, he had out of stock condition, twenty-two times, he had broken store displays, four times spilled milk, once rotten fruit, twice, blood in the meat packages and eighteen times, customer jam-ups at the checkstands. Obviously, his greatest single problem in the store is broken displays, the second is jam-ups at the checkstands and the third out of stock conditions. Rotten fruit and spilled milk are not problems that would necessarily disrupt the flow or operation of this store on a routine basis.

TAKING CARE OF THE GREATEST PROBLEMS FIRST

With this form of problem identification, we have a simple listing of the site conditions that did not appear correct and the action taken up on them. The exception information necessary to identify those problems to be resolved first is documented. In such fields as store management, in which the manager has probably come up from the working ranks of the organization, it becomes very difficult to distinguish the major problems from the minor ones. If, for example, the store manager started his career in the produce department, he quite naturally leans toward a neat, smoothly operating produce area, much more so than he would in, say, the meat department. But the impartial and objective singling out and documenting of problems forces a supervisor to identify those problems which require solution first, regardless of his predispositions. Failing such a discipline, a former produce manager would likely insist upon cleaning up the rotten fruit immediately, in spite of the fact that it was the lowest single incident problem. Taking care of the greatest problems first reflects the best utilization of labor and, ultimately, the best profitability. If, on the other hand, one fails to take care of those problems first, then labor can be far disproportionate to the results it should be achieving. This is particularly true in service type operations such as banks, airline ticket counters and grocery stores. In applying the techniques of the walking check and problem documentation, it must be borne in mind that the greatest problem is not always the easiest to identify. It is only through repeated and systematic use of this method that it will become evident, and very rapidly. The first walk through any operation is not going to identify what the major problems are, and so it is necessary to establish a routine and adhere to it, in order to pinpoint those problems through the repeated use of this method.

LEARNING TO CHECK ON THE PROBLEM SOLVING PROCESS

The top manager reviewing the check sheet has the advantage of seeing problems pinpointed and identified as they arise. In a large grocery chain employing the concept of Management by Exception and using the store supervisor's check sheet, the president made a practice of taking a walk with each supervisor some time during the course of the year. In one of these walks through a store that had been appreciably dropping in sales and increasing in labor, the president noted that the store supervisor made only two entries requiring correction. He asked the supervisor if he felt he had identified all the major problems he had seen, and the supervisor replied in the affirmative. A subsequent review of the supervisor's check sheets for the past few weeks revealed that he had never identified more than one or two problems, if, indeed, he had found any at all during the course of his walks. The president then requested the supervisor to take a walk through the store with him, while he himself made out the check sheet. The president's sheet noted four hundred items that required attention and were problems that existed in the store at that time. He knew how to check on the problem solving process to learn what the major problems in the store were. In the case of this particular store, the major problem was the supervisor's inability to identify those very problems that lay before him. By the completion of his four hundred exception items, the president had set an example for the supervisor so that when he walked the store in the future, he had a reference point from which to work. And the experience was equally enlightening for the president, who called all the district managers in to review his list, and they in turn used that list as reference points in the other stores.

Naturally, it would be impossible for presidents of companies this size to make detailed to-do lists for each operation, nor should they be expected to. But, by checking on the problem solving process itself, it was possible for this president to lay down a norm of performance expected. Higher managers have the responsibility of reviewing periodically the mechanics of their subordinates, to determine if they can identify problems. In many operations the woeful answer to shrinking profits, increasing labor costs and falling sales is, ''I don't see what's wrong.'' What the supervisor is really saying is, ''I don't have the vision necessary to see what's wrong,'' or ''My planning mechanism is failing me.'' In the case of the grocery chain, it was obvious that at no time did the plan include a standard of performance in the stores. In the past the plans had always included how many manhours should be used or how many dollars should be sold. The plan had never included how clean the floors should be or how well-stocked the shelves must appear.

FORMS THAT ASSIST IN DETERMINING THE BIG PROBLEMS

Many of the forms presented earlier (Figures 9, 10, 11, 12 and 13 specifically) can be used for line supervision implementation. In order to bring the problems and facts forward to top management, some interim forms are necessary, forms that assist in determining the big problems and focus those hourly, day to day departmental problems to give an overall picture necessary for decision making. Figure 15 shows an Exception Recap form that has almost universal application. It can be used in stores, shifts, departments and plants, depending on the reporting levels, and in several interim stages of reporting. For example, in a manufacturing complex composed of three plants, each having various departments, this form could be used throughout the entire system, with each department shift recapped in the plan. The areas might conceivably be sheet metal, first and second shifts, fabrication, first and second shifts, welding department, first

Exception Recap

Area	*Exceptions*											*Total*
	A	B	C	D	E	F	G	H	I	J	K	
Total												

FIGURE 15

and second shifts, painting department, first and second shifts, assembly department, first shift, and total. Once the daily method of problem identification through the tallying of exceptions to the plan is initiated, it is possible to strike off a plant exception recap. This, in turn, might be used in all three plants, so that, weekly, the production vice-president could have on his desk a recap of all the problems of all the plants of all the shifts of all the days of all the hours, and from that information he could determine specifically what his greatest single problem was. Figure 15 shows the flow of this kind of mechanism which would place the vice-president of production in receipt of the total information, not only of his three plants, but also of all his department foremen on all his shifts as well.

FAILURE TO IDENTIFY MAJOR EXCEPTIONS RETARDS GROWTH AND EXPANSION

What we are seeking in the use of Management by Exception Systems is, quite basically, that information we do not know. Such information tells us what must be done to improve. This simple truth is so often overlooked in so many companies. In Ford Motor Company's Edsel and Campbell Soup Company's Red Kettle line of soups, we have glaring examples of the failure to identify exceptions, retarding growth in certain product lines to a point at which the product no longer exists. Exceptions can occur in any of the disciplines one is dealing with, manufacturing, marketing, accounting, personnel, administration—any of them can be going off course and very probably because no one is identifying the exceptions. If, for example, a company planned to spend five thousand dollars a week on payroll, it would be important to note any major deviation from this figure; failure to note that the payroll had gone to seven thousand would very possibly dry up the cash and ruin the company. In order to know where to apply its decisions, management must constantly identify what exceptions are taking place in *all* of its disciplines. If it fails to identify major exceptions, time will be spent in putting out brush fires instead of expanding or showing a normal profit growth. It is vital, then, to identify those things which are not going according to plan. These items, once established, can usually be solved, but they can never be solved until they are identified.

MANAGEMENT BY EXCEPTION POINTERS

1. It is necessary to identify the greatest problems within an organization, and this can often best be done through information currently available. The manager should be wary of the more vocal complainers in his company.
2. An effective system will always pinpoint those problems of greatest magnitude.
3. Misdirected management drives can often result in wasted time and effort. It is futile to initiate such drives with inadequate or partial information.
4. Manpower reduction is not always the key to eliminating bad marketing conditions. Frequently, the manpower on hand can be redirected into more productive channels.
5. Major problems will often surface through the use of a simple supervisor's check sheet (see Figure 14) and a routing system of problem identification. Other forms (specifically Figures 9, 10, 11, 12 and 14) are useful at the line supervision level for identifying the bigger problems.

6

PITFALLS AND HUMAN FACTORS IN EMPLOYING MANAGEMENT BY EXCEPTION

"I DID IT, BUT IT DIDN'T WORK": THE FIRST TEST OF AN EXCEPTION SYSTEM

No exception system will long survive, unless the manager initiating it has sufficient confidence in his plan to repel the first attack from his subordinates, who will almost surely come running forward with the cry, ''I did it, but it didn't work.'' A subordinate's failure should in no way be the criterion for measuring either the validity of the plan or the system itself. Before accepting the ''I did it, but it didn't work'' answer, a manager must be certain he determines specifically *why* it didn't work; he must not accept blindly the subordinate's conclusions that it didn't—and therefore can't—work. In almost every case, such crepe hangers are the people of least experience; the greatest experience is found at the planning end, and, thus, it stands to reason that conclusions should be reached at the end.

WHY IT "DIDN'T WORK"

In trying to determine why the Management by Exception System ''didn't work,'' the manager always has the responsibility of eliminating the normal pitfalls and human frailties involved in the implementation of any new system.

Some of these fall into easily identifiable categories, such as lack of training, lack of equipment, lack of synchronization, lack of material and any of a host of other "lack of's." Whatever caused the system to go awry can usually be classed into a lack of something. Oftentimes, identification of just what is lacking can be difficult, as the shortage may have all the characteristics associated with the domino theory. For example, the lack of material at an assembly line might have been caused by the lack of equipment to transport it, which, in turn, was caused by the lack of trained personnel to drive that equipment. All of these missing elements come into play. The manager's problem may be compounded by the fact that problems existing two or three departments away are not readily apparent to the individual declaring that the system "didn't work." In earlier chapters we discussed the categorization of exceptions, as well as the consolidating and bringing forward the magnitude of the several categories to the top manager. Only in this way was it possible to determine what precisely was the cause of production failure. Because of the fundamental unreliability of the human element, cross checks for the manager and the system must be established before that system can be committed to execution.

CROSS CHECKS FOR THE MANAGER AND THE SYSTEM

The surest and easiest cross check to use in a Management by Exception System is the transposition of materials or work from one format to another. An example of this would be an office in which input is measured in invoices and output is recorded in standard hours of production. Suppose you are interested in determining how many standard hours are produced by the production of, say, 1500 invoices. To do so, you would make a cross audit of one tally or count as it compares with the other. Don't be too surprised to find that the tallies initially don't agree. Most seasoned managers, whether they use a formal Management by Exception System or not, have learned to use some basic rules of thumb to guide them in cross checking the flow of their systems, as it moves toward the pay point. Examples of this can be seen in manufacturers who, regardless of the complexity of their accounting system, still go back and count the number of condensers entered into flow each day or how many pounds of plastic were consumed the night before or how many skids were placed in the warehouse. In such cases, the manager instinctively uses a double method of cross checks to determine the accuracy of the reports in front of him. Or, put more simply, he is cross checking his own system so that if he is confronted with a problem, he has already made the determination of its magnitude as well as its validity.

TWO CASES IN POINT

A. A large jewelry manufacturer and retailer, operating nationally, made it a point to have on his desk each Monday morning a report of his entire operation.

This report was a composite of all of his 900 retail outlets, as well as his various distribution warehouses throughout the United States. During one period, it became evident that the dollar sales were deteriorating on a week to week basis. Because this particular manager had built cross checks into his system and was noting the exceptions, he moved quickly to follow the flow of the units shipped out of each of his distribution warehouses. A cross check of his dollar sales and his warehouse distribution soon revealed a most perplexing problem. While his sales were decreasing, the units shipped to his warehouse outlets were on the increase. The manager performed the usual audit to check the mathematics, and he did some selective sampling to determine whether normal human frailties in the reporting mechanism were the cause of what seemed to be an impossible situation. On very short inspection it soon became apparent, that a slight recession was in progress across the country, and initially it affected adversely retail jewelry sales. At the same time, however, people had not stopped patronizing the men's stores; they had merely stopped buying the higher priced items and had moved to those less expensive, the net result of which was to increase the actual work content or volume of the stores, while decreasing their dollar sales. Armed with this information, the manager was able to change his marketing approach to fit the new economic condition. That year, he showed his shareholders their greatest profits ever, while his competitors were still puzzled by what appeared to be conflicting information. The reason his competitors failed to take advantage of this change in the marketing picture was their inability to build cross checks into their systems. In effect, they failed to realize that further management investigation is often required on specific data fed into those systems.

B. A second case—again involving warehousing and retail selling—in which the system did not serve management and did not signal a change in work content as well as requirements, is a retail plumbing hardware, safety equipment and building supply warehouse in Honolulu, Hawaii. In this example, an ostensibly good operating system informed management of after-the-fact results of line items shipped and dollars sold in the retail-wholesale warehouse. During peak volume management was always alerted to the fact that more labor was needed to meet customer requirements and maintain a certain standard of customer service. However, the system did not have cross checks which would warn management of the deterioration of line items shipped and dollar volume, which, in fact, increased the necessary labor required in the warehouse itself. As the warehouse increased its sales of about 1,000 line items, or $5,000 per month, management readily added labor to take care of the growing volume. But, when this business trend was reversed due to a shipping strike, the system did not alert management to the fact that as volume decreased, the labor content of order filling increased.

The reason, once resolved, was relatively simple. As volume increased, each invoice or customer order had approximately 13 line items to be filled. This meant that an employee might walk the length and breadth of the warehouse and select 13 items in his box and return to the customer counter. The labor content, then, was the total walking of the warehouse divided into 13 selected items. Since there was no cross check in the system reflecting the relationship between invoices or customer orders and line items to be selected, it was not noted, that as the volume dropped, the individual order selector would walk the entire length of the warehouse for what now amounted to 4 line items per customer order. Thus, the distance traveled by an individual employee increased by something over 300%. Because of this increase, it became virtually impossible for the employee to fill customer orders as the volume continued to drop. Before management became deeply involved, a back order situation, that was all but disasterous, had been created. While the reporting system continued to reflect a reduction of sales items and sales dollars, the telephones rang more frequently with angry customers denouncing the bad customer service at the warehouse dock. This situation grew to dangerous proportions, until management, through careful inspection at the line level, was able to determine that the labor content had actually increased as the volume was reduced. It took better than a year to recover the loss of dollar volume occasioned by irritated customers and poor service. And the initial gains made through an operating system, which lacked cross checks, were more than offset by the bad marketing posture and loss of future business that resulted.

HOW TO DIFFERENTIATE HUMAN FRAILTIES FROM SYSTEMS PROBLEMS

One of the simplest methods used to differentiate between human frailties, that cause a system to function improperly, and an actual problem inherent in the system itself, is the matter of exceptions. When exceptions cease to be identified, almost without fail, the manager can look directly to human frailties involved in his system. Consider some of the examples we have cited previously. The store supervisor walks his store purposely to discover exceptions to the plan he laid out the prior week. When his sheet comes back time and again with no exceptions recorded and still the use of manpower is in excess of his plan, or customer service has failed to meet the standards management has established, then he has tied his problem directly to the operator or operators in the system, rather than to the system itself. Similarly, a sales system in which sales reports come in, volume upon volume, ream upon ream, and, yet, no reasons for failures to make sales are noted, also signals a failure of the operators of that system. What has been identified is not a sales problem, but a human problem. The first and perhaps most important rule, then, in differentiating between human frailties and systems problems is the failure of the system to function at all (this assumes, of course, the system is one of Management by Exception). Many systems of planning, executing and reporting may be sound, but, if they lack the element of exception reporting, they have built into them the seeds of their own failures in achieving consistent improvement. It is necessary to continuously identify problems in order to improve, revise and increase the productivity of Management by Exception Systems.

A manager on a large vehicle maintenance project once asked the designer of a Management by Exception System, "How long must I use this system before I won't have to worry about all these exceptions?" The systems designer's answer was, "Until the day you retire." He understood that the day he failed to identify exceptions was the day they no longer needed him or his expertise in the management of that operation. This fact is often overlooked by managers, for there is a *natural human tendency to want to solve a problem and then reap the benefits of the solution, rather than to move on quickly to the next problem.*

While a failure to identify problems or exceptions is almost a sure indication of human frailties involved in the system, a failure of the system to produce results is just as surely an indication of its own weakness. Thus, when problems or exceptions are identified and the plan to use manpower and material is going reasonably well, and, yet, the desired results are still not achieved, one must re-examine the system, searching for inherent flaws inadvertently built into it.

CASE IN POINT

A well known specialty truck manufacturer in the Pacific Northwest developed a system of planning that emphasized heavily controls at the execution level and reporting. Initially, its implementation brought some dramatic results; there was no disputing the fact, that, in the first week and a half of operation, the productivity of the individual employees was substantially increased. However, the possibility of inherent weaknesses in the system or of its failure had not been taken into consideration. By the end of the second week, the top managers' cheeriness had turned to gloom. It was discovered that, true to the predicitons of the system's designers, each unit was produced with an impressive 22% decrease in manhours from before. But, the designers had failed to account for the fact, that no matter how well 30 units were produced per week (as against the 45 that had been produced in the past), the 30 were not sufficient to carry the overhead of the sales force, the production plant, the clerical staff and other support groups. In this instance, the system itself had failed to consider the volume production necessary to cover the overhead. The emphasis had been directly on the use of manpower, and the reports coming in showed dramatic improvement but failed, through any cross check or audit, to detect the system's major flaw: enough units were simply not being produced to cover the overhead.

It is interesting to note that the perfection of the system becomes your first indication of either a failure through human frailties or through the system itself.

To review once more: when the system shows no exceptions whatsoever, and the desired results are not achieved, you have a general indication that you are dealing with some personnel or human problems. On the other hand, when the system balances, identifies problems, proceeds according to plan, and the results are still not achieved, you generally have an indication that an inherent weakness exists within the system. In both cases, a well designed and implemented system of Management by Exception is needed, with a good plan in place prior to moving to the execution phase, with provision on a routine basis for a detailing of the exceptions and with a reporting mechanism that will move upward to put vital data in the hands of decision making management—all of these elements will provide for the differentiation between human frailties and systems problems.

GIVING THE SYSTEM A FAIR TEST

Perhaps the surest method of avoiding rejection of any system in its early stages is a clear, concise directive from top management, indicating that the system, though imperfect, will be modified until it operates successfully. After three months of design, implementation, adjusting and re-tuning of a Management by Exception system, a Gulf states shipping firm called together all of its department managers and had each one explain the planning, executing, excepting and reporting mechanisms, both as they applied specifically to his department, and as they related generally to the entire operation. The sales manager began and, for the first time, people at the operations level realized that they were directly affected by the successful execution of the sales plan. Next, the operations manager reviewed his planning mechanism from the moment of a committed sale through the detailing of the operation. He reviewed the method which signaled any imminent problems, the identification of recurring problems for solution and the ultimate reporting and planning improvement mechanism.

The comptroller of the organization was given the assignment of explaining the support Management by Exception System as it applied to the whole. After discussing the basic mechanics of the system, he told a personal story of his imprisonment on the island of Java during the Second World War by the Japanese. He explained that, as the war continued, the rations of food grew shorter and shorter, and the inmates of the prison camp began to die of starvation. Several of the inmates devised a plan to smuggle in food and to allow some of the prisoners to escape, but there were critics who pointed out the plan's weakness and hazards, so convincingly it seemed, that the plan was not immediately executed. At that point, as the comptroller put it, the prisoners had the choice between dying and dying. After a pause he added, "When confronted with this choice, we decided to execute the plan regardless of the hazards." Within a few short weeks, the Japanese guards were asking why none had died recently in the camp. The comptroller's answer to the group? "The plan may not have been perfect, but it was executed willingly."

This simple, illustrative story emphasized the surest method of avoiding rejection of a system in its early stages. That method is top management, middle management and line supervision endorsement of the ultimate goals the plan is attempting to achieve. Naturally, it is convenient to be able to point pridefully at the success of the system in another company or department, but that of itself is rarely enough to avoid rejection in the early stages, particularly by those at the execution or line level. Prior to committing your company to any system, management should carefully walk through the system, comparing it with whatever is currently in place.

All levels of management should be thoroughly convinced that the new system will work, regardless of adjustments that may be required in putting it into place. Once this determination has been made, management should communicate to all levels of the operation the results of the check; they should indicate their faith in the validity of the system, and they should explain their provision for cross checks, which will indicate when corrections are needed. In addition, management must stay reasonably close to the system during its early stages in order to provide the necessary counsel and guidance. If management tries to implement an exception system through decree and without charging the subordinate managers with the responsibility of further detailing the plan to set into place the very mechanism necessary to identify exceptions, then the system has a lessened chance of success. Simply stated, the method of avoiding rejection of a system in its early stages lies in the hands of management and in its own attitude toward the success of the system. What is required is a clear indication to all levels of the operation that the system, while certainly not perfect in the beginning, will be implemented, and that necessary adjustments will be taken after sufficient time has elapsed to identify *systems* problems—not those caused by lack of training, lack of material, human frailties or any others which might arise in the course of the systems implementation. If, during the implementation of a new system, anywhere along the chain of command, a manager is allowed the attitude of "It can't be done," then, most assuredly, that system will be in for some tough sledding before it becomes a way of life for the employees charged with its operation.

TWO CASES IN POINT

A. A large personnel department in a Chicago-based oil company had a Management by Exception System implemented in its department, as well as throughout the company. One young personnel manager thought it an affront to his intelligence to have to work within the framework of a routine problem documenting, planning, executing and reporting system. His exception system proved to be such a thorn in his side, that he went out of his way to prove that "it can't be done." His method was to work within the confines of the system itself, to exaggerate the problems, to blow them out of proportion and to document the minutest detail of every single incidence of exceptions, until management was confronted with an almost insurmountable preponderance of evidence that the system was responsible for creating many of the exceptions themselves. His zeal to disprove the validity of the system was ultimately his undoing, for the conclusions that came forward to top management of the company pinpointed the loss of production caused by 143 phone call interruptions, 29 special interviews, 14 projects, and so on *ad infinitum*. Management applied a time value to each of these exceptions, so laboriously listed by the young manager, and quickly found that he was interrupted more than the 40 hours per week he was working. His attempt to document the unimportant, the incidental, cost him his job, as the management of this firm was committed to the success of the system. In its early stages they had walked it through and given it their full support, so fully in fact, that they were unimpressed by an insubordiante means of an exaggerated use of the system itself.

B. In a large construction company it is essential that the trucks carrying the various building materials arrive on time. In one such company a Management by Exception System was initiated. The plan called for fine synchronization in the dispatching of the materials trucks from a mid-point between the construction site and the source of the material supplies. The system originally had involved management; it provided for the identification and documentation of exceptions and allowed for the auditing and correcting of any problems that might arise. At the end of the third day, the documentation reflected an abnormally large loss of manpower due to poor synchronization of truck arrival, which was an astonishing development, in view of the fact the system was designed precisely to avoid that situation. This system seemed to prove, on the surface at least, that it could not work. Step by step, the plans were reviewed by the managers responsible for detailing the various levels. Everything appeared to be sound. Yet, on the fourth day the documentation reflected even more of the same. It was not until the system was abandoned, and the old method of dispatching revived, that someone, in reviewing the results, noted that there was a predictable amount of time built into the delay of the trucks in arriving at the work stations. This situation aroused the curiosity of one manager, who proceeded to review every element of the system. He discovered that several standard data sheets had been developed for the time required to dispatch a truck from the materials point to the proper area at the construction site. Quite simply, what had happened was that the dispatcher had picked up the wrong standard data sheet and was dispatching trucks to an entirely different construction site. Once this had been identified, the correct standard data sheet was inserted, the system was re-instituted and the desired results were immediately achieved. In this case, the system of Management by Exception proved to be its own undoing when it was turned back on itself, audited, reviewed, cross checked and still found to be wanting. No one had thought during the course of all this to check the simplest element of all, the standard data which was used to dispatch the trucks.

OVERCOMPENSATION DUE TO EXAGGERATED REPORTING

Almost everyone in the business world knows of departments or areas that are overstaffed because of their supervisors' exaggerations of the ''killing'' work loads. An interesting example of this sort of situation was found in the national headquarters of a large snack company located in Dallas, Texas. The central file department had a reputation for being one of the most efficient, well-run departments in the company. When a new system of Management by Exception was introduced into this area, a volume tally was initiated in order to determine the input and the output of the department over a two month period. Simultaneously with the tally, standards were developed for the department in order to indicate the manpower required at various volume levels. It should be noted that the work load in the department was of such a repetitive, routine nature that not very many standards were required, and it was a relatively simple area to bring under the system's control.

Figure 16 illustrates the plotting in number of manhours required each day, that is, the input/output work load. The measurement, a two month plotting, took place from February 18, through April 17. At times, the volume requirement dropped as low as 20 hours for the department; at other times it rose as high as 110. These conditions posed a perplexing problem, for the employees worked an eight hour day, and, yet, the work requirement dropped as low as a need for 2-1/2 persons at one point and rose to as high as a need for 14 at another. The file department had a reputation for getting work out on demand, and so it was necessary to maintain this service for the rest of the company. The graph would indicate, then, that it would be relatively insecure to drop the department anywhere below its average number of hours required, which figure was around eight people. Still, one of the primary goals of the system was to eliminate unnecessary hours, and the problem seemed impossible of solution. It remained for the systems manager to discover that overcompensation, due to exaggerated reporting, was at the root of the apparent dilemma. In reviewing the data that had been used to load the department, he noted that when a stack of papers came in, the supervisor would count every page, even though those papers were stapled and were to be filed in a single location. That was his first discovery: literally every sheet of paper that passed into and through the department was counted.

VOLUME IN REQUIRED WORK HOURS

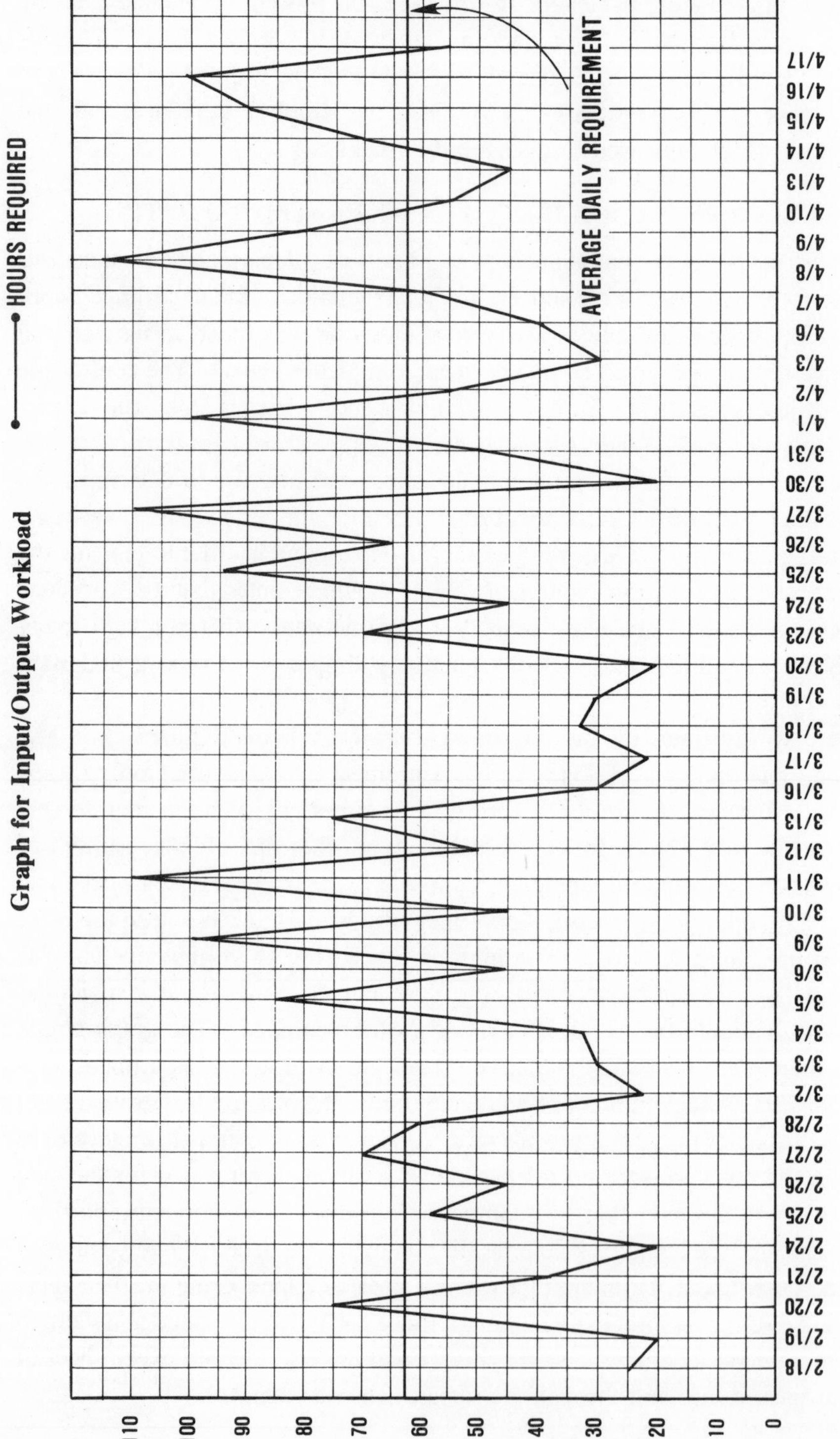

FIGURE 16

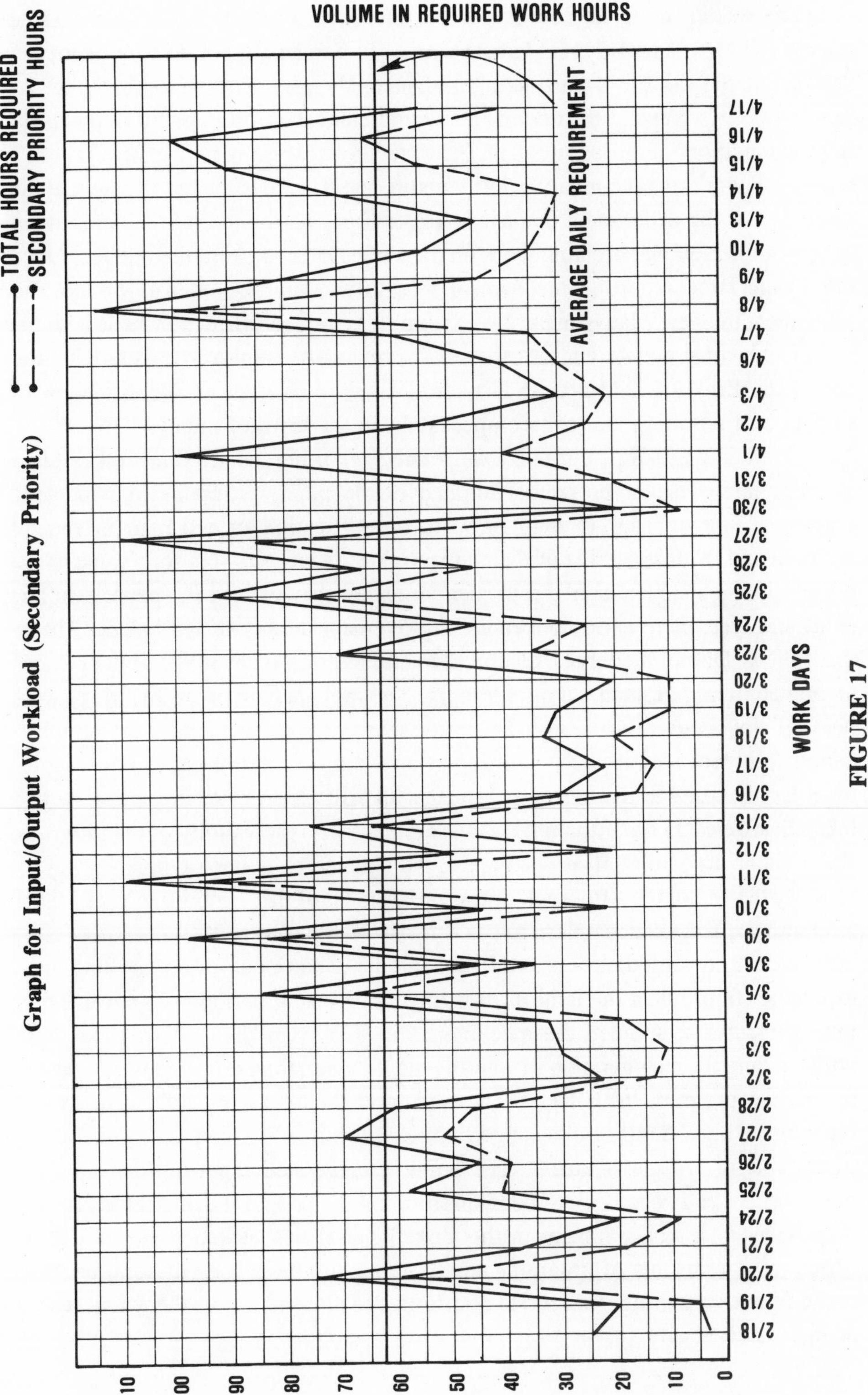
Graph for Input/Output Workload (Secondary Priority)
TOTAL HOURS REQUIRED
SECONDARY PRIORITY HOURS
VOLUME IN REQUIRED WORK HOURS
AVERAGE DAILY REQUIREMENT
110
100
90
80
70
60
50
40
30
20
10
0
2/18
2/19
2/20
2/21
2/24
2/25
2/26
2/27
2/28
3/2
3/3
3/4
3/5
3/6
3/9
3/10
3/11
3/12
3/13
3/16
3/17
3/18
3/19
3/20
3/23
3/24
3/25
3/26
3/27
3/30
3/31
4/1
4/2
4/3
4/6
4/7
4/8
4/9
4/10
4/13
4/14
4/15
4/16
4/17
WORK DAYS

FIGURE 17

The second thing he noted was that all work was handled with the same priority. Thus, if a presidential letter agreeing to purchase a potato chip factory in Seattle entered the file department simultaneously with the tri-monthly issue of the *Potato Chip News*, both documents would enter the filing system at precisely the same number of lapsed minutes. Priorities, then, were nonexistent (Figure 17 reflects all work of a secondary priority nature, work to be attended to solely at the discretion of the department manager). In addition, he found that the department supervisor herself was creating work on days of peak input from the outside. Once this exaggerated reporting mechanism was fully identified, it was possible to implement the new Management by Exception system in this department with the use of only four people and not the eight previously employed. This reduction netted the firm $32,000 a year in payroll savings through an identification of exaggerated reporting and overcompensation in the form of manpower.

Overcompensation, through exaggerated reporting, many times takes place in work improvement programs initiated in the plant, programs in which the employees are enlisted to help in work simplification or work improvement methods and the formalizing of their supervision. In cases of this sort, some of the alleged savings are exaggerated to such an extent they exceed the payroll dollars paid, and, yet, there is no noticeable improvement on any of the balance sheets that follow. One of the largest electrical manufacturing firms in the United States attempted to initiate such a program in its food appliance division. Meetings were held religiously each week, and discussion of work improvement, work simplification, problem identification and reporting went on interminably. Each supervisor would come to the meetings armed with written proof of the action he had taken that week. In order to impress management with the validity of the program, the initiator urged that all needed action be equated to dollar savings.

By the end of the fifth week of this program all of the ''improvements'' (such as shutting off hot water unless it was actually being used and having lower class labor clean and wash dies sent to the tool and die department for repair) amounted to a larger figure than the total payroll for the reporting period. Not surpisingly, management discontinued the meetings. The sorry part of it all was that, notwithstanding the exaggeration of improvement by equating it to imaginary dollars saved, the program itself had been valid, and the improvements were in fact creating savings. Savings of a longer range sort, however, were not immediately discernible to top management. The point: Exaggerated reporting can result in both positive and negative overcompensation by the people reading those reports. Almost every major company in the United States has tucked away in a dusty office those remnants of programs and systems that have been discontinued because of over reporting, inaccurate reporting or failure to report the actual results of the system itself.

Another form of exaggerated reporting is often reflected in some of the forms presented in previous chapters. Form 9 shows ten predetermined categories as causes of lost production. A paper box manufacturing company in Vancouver, Canada, once used this method of Management by Exception reporting to identify causes of lost production on its operating floor. Its printing presses, its cutting machines and its paper box manufacturing all initiated an exception reporting system, but unfortunately, no one had thought to categorize the causes of lost production.

After three weeks of implementation of the system, over 300 different reasons for lost production emerged. At this point, management entered into the system, was confronted with literally reams of paper explaining the various reasons (none of which had any apparent relation to another), threw up their hands in despair and ordered the removal of the exception reporting aspect of the system. The sad part of that decision was that the very exception reporting itself might have led that management to improvement. Eventually, troubleshooting systems men were brought in from the United States, and they quickly identified the problem: overcompensation due to exaggerated reporting at *both* ends of the chain of command. The top management had insisted that they discontinue the exception reporting system, while those at the line operating level were maintaining they were spending more time writing about the problems than they were in solving them. This situation had a happy ending: limited categories were quickly established; the wheat was removed from the chaff; the exaggerated reporting system was discontinued; management re-instituted the causes for lost production; management pinpointed many major problems in the plant; and today the same plant operates with a work force reduced by 21% and with an annual production increase of over 12%. The dollar savings amounted to well over half a million per year. Yet, the system came dangerously close to being discarded because of overcompensation due to exaggerated reporting.

What forms, then, can be employed that will audit themselves and prevent human error negligence?

FORMS THAT AUDIT THEMSELVES

In considering forms that will audit themselves against human error and negligence, one must remember that, in order to institute any Management by Exception System, it is important to have the facts in place before developing the system itself. For this reason the necessary audit forms fall into two categories: the tally or documentation of statistics as they currently exist, and the form that reflects volume of statistical data after it has been gathered, that is, the form for a routine, continuing operation.

Figure 18 illustrates an example of the simplest form of a volume tally. It lists the activities or major headings of the activities of a department or operation, and it allows the supervisor or clerk charged with the responsibility to tally the number of units to be processed each day and to total them at the end of the week. Many times, such a form will be entirely sufficient for the operation. If, however, there can be any misunderstanding, further information may be needed in advance (you recall the example of the pages that were counted instead of the actual incidents of filing), and it may be necessary to add a unit of measure memorandum to the form. In addition, in using the volume tally it may sometimes be important to differentiate between input and output, in order for the supervisor to see quite clearly when an imbalance is occuring and to level his work load. A

Volume Tally

ACTIVITY	MONDAY	TUESDAY	WEDNESDAY	THURSDAY	FRIDAY	TOTAL
TYPE LETTERS	卌 II	卌	II	卌 卌 卌 II	卌 卌 卌	46
STUFF ENVELOPES	卌 III	IIII	卌 卌	卌	–	27
DRAFT FORMS	II	III	I			6

FIGURE 18

backlog report or carry-over information at the end of a week may also be significant. Whatever embellishments or additions may be needed are best illustrated by taking Figure 18 and expanding it into what now appears in Figure 19. Here we have taken the simple stenographic tally and expanded it into a manager's report on carryover input and output, a report that nails down the unit of measure. This same technique can be used regardless of what the activity or the desired tally figures are—cases, pounds, dollars, invoices, whatever information the manager is after.

Sometimes the item to be tallied or audited could take the form of customer service. Figure 20 illustrates a large supermarket in which the customers and the dollars, by specific checkstand and time of day, are tallied. In the use of these

Volume Tally Expanded to Manager's Report on Carryover Input/Output

ACTIVITY	UNIT OF MEASURE	MON (IN / OUT)	TUES (IN / OUT)	WED (IN / OUT)	THUR (IN / OUT)	FRI (IN / OUT)	SAT (IN / OUT)	WEEK TOTAL	CARRY OVER
TYPE LETTERS	FULL PAGE	15 / 7	10 / 5	8 / 2	12 / 17	25 / 15	0 / 0	70 / 46	24
STUFF ENVELOPES	ENVELOPE	27 / 8	– / 4	– / 10	– / 5	– / 0	– / 0	27 / 27	0
DRAFT FORMS	FULL PAGE	16 / 2	– / 3	– / 1	– / 0	– / 0	– / 0	16 / 6	10

FIGURE 19

Customer Dollar Recap

DATE: A.M. P.M. STORE:

Time	*Customers Sales $*	*Checkstand Numbers* 1	2	3	4	5	6	7	8	9	10	*Total*
1200	Customers											
0100	Dollars											
0100	Customers											
0200	Dollars											
0200	Customers											
0300	Dollars											
0300	Customers											
0400	Dollars											
0400	Customers											
0500	Dollars											
0500	Customers											
0600	Dollars											
0600	Customers											
0700	Dollars											
0700	Customers											
0800	Dollars											
0800	Customers											
0900	Dollars											
0900	Customers											
1000	Dollars											
1000	Customers											
1100	Dollars											
1100	Customers											
1200	Dollars											

FIGURE 20

forms, it must be remembered that the purpose is always to document what the volume, the manhours, the dollars, the pounds and the invoices are prior to the implementation of any new system, particularly one of Management by Exception. Many times in implementing a new system, an attempt is made to overlay that system without adequate knowledge of the volume fluctuations on an hour-to-hour, day-to-day basis. Forms that audit themselves against human error and negligence are usually those that have been designed after a sufficiently long period of tallies of input and output have been measured, as illustrated in Figures 18, 19 and 20. Therefore, regardless of the complexity of the form or the particular volume requirements the firm is attempting to capture, such data has to be gathered prior to moving on to the second group of forms, which will become a part of a Management by Exception System. An earlier form, Figure 12, exemplifies a clerical flow report that uses the information as developed in either Figures 18 or 19, placing that data into effect on assigned work loads after the volume tally has been secured over a reasonable length of time. The volume tallies developed would then be used to load the various employees and provide sufficient hours to complete the work load, while at the same time noting that the backlog or carry-over is not increasing.

Now the auditing method is in place. Should the employee forget to note the amount entering the work flow, or should he exaggerate the amount that is complete, the volume tally secured before the implementation of the new system can quickly be matched against it, and the supervisor is, by exception to the pattern established, apprised of the work flow. None of this purports to be a substitute for actual supervision at the right time; it merely demonstrates, that by using such an audit, one will know in advance what the picture *should* be, for the manager or supervisor can see by exception that the established pattern is not now occurring. This is not to say that valid changes in the work input or output cannot happen, but it does mean that on a day-to-day basis, that pattern will be brought into focus.

A more complex method of using an initial tally is found in Figure 20, which is taken into a computer and followed by Figure 21, a printout by the computer of the data as it was tallied at the store level. This system provides a permanent record of the customer and dollar pattern to be established. If one is dealing with a particularly large group of stores over a long period of time, this data, handled by a computer, enables the top management of the firm to note any changes in the pattern of the entire chain, division, region or particular store itself during any given hour, day, week or month.

Figure 22 reflects a total Management by Exception System, which now equates basic volume as developed in Figure 20 on through the simple printing of the conclusions, and takes it a step further by equating it to customer service and checking requirements. Using this set of illustrations, we can see how a system may be audited. For instance, when a manager walks into a store and finds customers waiting, he can quickly pull his data processing form, developed as you will recall from the checkstand readings themselves, and see if the supervisor of the store has provided the necessary checkstands. Once again, this brings a very complex operation, one with much diversity of geography, hours of the day, days of the week and weeks of the month, into focus, so that a manager can, by exception note if the problem is a systems problem or one of human error and negligence. These forms are not intended to be all-inclusive, but they are examples of methods of determining in advance what the facts are before a system is implemented. Through their use human error and negligence can be distinguished from improper systems design, and management can be brought into the flow to take corrective action.

Customer-Dollar Pattern

CUSTOMER & DOLLAR RECAP

PURPOSE: To provide a summary of the Customer Count and Dollar Volume by store, by hour, so that trends are highlighted and buying patterns recognized. Pinpoints high volume times during the day for Total Dollars and Customers, and Dollars per Customer.

HOW TO READ THE RECAP: The Recap is intended to show hourly, daily and weekly operation of the store. Below is an explanation of the information on the Recap.

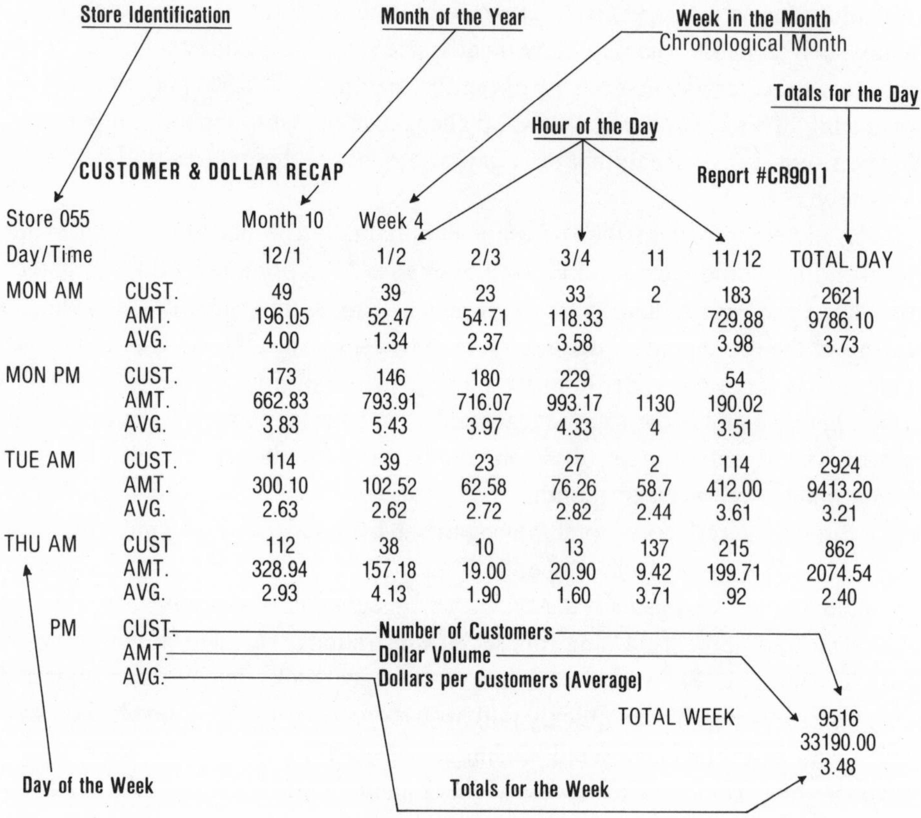

CUSTOMER & DOLLAR RECAP

Report #CR9011

Store 055		Month 10	Week 4					
Day/Time		12/1	1/2	2/3	3/4	11	11/12	TOTAL DAY
MON AM	CUST.	49	39	23	33	2	183	2621
	AMT.	196.05	52.47	54.71	118.33		729.88	9786.10
	AVG.	4.00	1.34	2.37	3.58		3.98	3.73
MON PM	CUST.	173	146	180	229		54	
	AMT.	662.83	793.91	716.07	993.17	1130	190.02	
	AVG.	3.83	5.43	3.97	4.33	4	3.51	
TUE AM	CUST.	114	39	23	27	2	114	2924
	AMT.	300.10	102.52	62.58	76.26	58.7	412.00	9413.20
	AVG.	2.63	2.62	2.72	2.82	2.44	3.61	3.21
THU AM	CUST	112	38	10	13	137	215	862
	AMT.	328.94	157.18	19.00	20.90	9.42	199.71	2074.54
	AVG.	2.93	4.13	1.90	1.60	3.71	.92	2.40
PM	CUST.							
	AMT.							
	AVG.							

TOTAL WEEK	
	9516
	33190.00
	3.48

FIGURE 21

Total Management by Exception System

Aid to Planning

Source Data for Checkstand Crewing Guide

Customer Service Standard Data Store Number: 2-8-17 DATE:						
STAFFING COMBINATIONS	Customers Processed per Hour by Sales Dollar per Customer Ranges					
	$0.00-$2.99	$3.00-$3.99	$4.00-$4.49	$4.50-$4.99	$5.00-$5.49	$5.50-up
Customers Processed per Hour						
CASHIER CHECKING WITH CLERK HELPER BAGGING AT TWO TO THREE CHECKSTANDS	54	50	48	46	43	40
CASHIER CHECKING WITH NO CLERK HELPER	38	35	34	31	30	28
Customers Processed per Hour						
CUSTOMERS PROCESSED PER HOUR BY A CLERK HELPER	150	120	110	100	90	75

Type of Checkout Equipment
REGISTER- SWEDA SCALE- SLIDING CHECKSTAND- CUSTOMER PARTICIPATION

FIGURE 22

EXAMPLES OF SUPERVISOR MISUNDERSTANDING

Somewhere between human error, negligence and actual system failure lies that elusive area of supervisor misunderstanding. This is not always easy to determine, as few people care to admit their ignorance, and worse, oftentimes, they are unaware of it. Therefore, any person implementing any system, particularly one of Management by Exception, must realize that people will nod their heads and say, "I understand," when in fact, they are baffled. For this reason implementation of the system can be accomplished only with careful training of the man charged with the responsibility of supervision. The most effective method is the slow, step by step introduction of the supervisor into the elements of the system. That being so, it is necessary to review what those elements are. Facts, in the form of standard data sheets, former volume tallies, due dates, levels of customer service or standards of performance must all be carefully reviewed, documented and thoroughly covered prior to the first move into any new system. Many times, the supervisor is woefully ignorant of not only the manpower consumed, but also of the volume flow through his operation, the due date required, the customer service expected by his management and the original standards of performance as well. All of these elements may have eluded him as he became involved in the day-to-day mechanics and flow of his operation. Thus, these basic elements must be standardized.

Figure 23 demonstrates the formalization of some ostensibly obvious activities. This particular illustration was taken after the implementation of a Management by Exception System in a large automotive maintenance garage. Initially, the supervisor resisted the system because he simply did not know what the work activities were. In the past he had always been told through a work order exactly what was required for each automobile. Under the new system he was expected not only to do as he had before, but also to begin planning for the future, in order to call out crewing requirements.

Since labor was becoming a critical item with this firm, the management found it necessary to know when the work loads would lag sufficiently to commit personnel to a building program currently underway. There was no other labor available in this community, and any extra labor had to be found within the regular work force. The supervisor resisted because the basic element of the system was missing: he literally did not know on a formal basis the work that was expected of him. He had never had a volume tally (such as illustrated in Figure 18), which enumerated on a regular basis how many times brakes were overhauled, say, or how many times the front spindle on the field equipment was re-bushed. Because this fundamental tally was lacking, there was no automotive garage standard data, and, of course, no consequent equation of work to time. Once the automotive garage tallies were introduced and equated by industrial

Automotive Garage Standard Data

Activity	*Frequency*	*Unit of Measure*	*Units Per Hour*	*Hours Per Unit*
Overhaul Brakes - Auto.	Backlog	Brakes	.3	4.0
Overhaul Brakes - Truck, Trailer	Backlog	Brakes	.2	6.0
Repair Steering Components - Auto.	Backlog	Components	.2	6.0
Repair Steering Components - Truck	Backlog	Components	.1	8.0
Repair Steering Components - Fld. Equip.	Backlog	Components	-	12.0
Re-Bush Front Spindle - Auto.	Backlog	Spindle	.1	8.0
Re-Bush Front Spindle - Truck	Backlog	Spindle	.1	8.0
Re-Bush Front Spindle - Fld. Equip.	Backlog	Spindle	.1	8.0
Repair/Replace Springs - Auto.	Backlog	Spring	.3	3.0
Repair/Replace Springs - Truck/Trailer	Backlog	Spring	.1	8.0
Replace Exhaust System Comp. - Auto.	Backlog	Components	.5	2.0
Replace Exhaust System Comp. - Truck	Backlog	Components	.5	3.0
Replace Exhaust Sys. Comp. - Fld. Equip.	Backlog	Components	.3	3.0
Replace Exhaust Sys. Comp. - Aux. Equip.	Backlog	Components	.5	2.0
Repair Cooling System - Auto.	Backlog	System	1.0	1.0
Repair Cooling System - Truck	Backlog	System	.7	1.5
Repair Cooling System - Fld. Equip.	Backlog	System	.5	2.0
Repair Cooling System - Aux. Equip.	Backlog	System	.5	2.0
Replace Fuel System/Gas - Auto.	Backlog	System	1.0	1.0
Replace Fuel System/Gas - Truck	Backlog	System	1.0	1.0
Replace Fuel System/Gas - Fld. Equip.	Backlog	System	1.0	1.0
Replace Fuel System/Gas - Aux. Equip.	Backlog	System	1.0	1.0
Replace Fuel System/Diesel - Truck	Backlog	System	.3	3.0
Replace Fuel Sys./Diesel - Fld. Equip.	Backlog	System	.3	3.0
Replace Fuel Sys./Diesel - Aux. Equip.	Backlog	System	.5	2.0
R/R Electric System - Auto.	Backlog	System	.3	4.0
R/R Electric System - Truck	Backlog	System	.3	4.0
R/R Electric System - Trailer	Backlog	System	.2	6.0
R/R Electric System - Field Equip.	Backlog	System	.2	6.0
R/R Electric System - Aux. Equip.	Backlog	System	.7	1.5
R/R Fender - Auto.	Backlog	Fender	.5	2.0
Repair Body - Auto.	Backlog	Body	-	40.0
R/R Fender - Truck	Backlog	Fender	.3	3.0
Repair Body - Truck	Backlog	Body	-	40.0
R/R Fender - Field Equipment	Backlog	Fender	.3	3.0
Repair Body - Field Equipment	Backlog	Body	-	40.0
Replace Dash Instruments - Auto.	Backlog	Instrument	.5	2.0
Replace Dash Instruments - Truck	Backlog	Instrument	.5	2.0
Replace Dash Instruments - Fld. Equip.	Backlog	Instrument	.5	2.0
Replace Dash Instruments - Aux. Equip.	Backlog	Instrument	.5	2.0

FIGURE 23

engineers to reasonably workable time for planning purposes, the supervisor was able to tell management exactly how much labor would be available on a week-to-week basis. By taking care of the first element of the system, the documentation of facts, and by placing those facts in the form of aids, this firm freed 67 people from all the various shops and was able to build a 2-1/2 million dollar capital project with that labor.

But far from having to spend any additional payroll, this firm had made a $536,000 annual payroll reduction, either in the maintenance garage or the capital project, wherever the accountants put it.

It is necessary, then, to nail down the facts for the supervisors, so there can be no misunderstanding of the first elements to be used. The succeeding steps, planning, executing, identifying exceptions and reporting them back to management will follow naturally. Since supervisory misunderstanding generally involves an ignorance of the facts as they exist, the systems designer has a responsibility to document, formalize and prepare all such necessary facts for review at all levels of supervision. Of course, the supervisor may not understand the use of these facts. Often, this involves an imperfect understanding of why the system requires certain documentation at a certain time. An example of this, in which the implement of the system was himself at fault, was a cryogenics plant in northern Texas. Here, the standard data appeared as an industrial engineer's time and motion study rather than as a supervisory tool.

The cylinder testing and painting department was involved. The flow consisted of returned oxygen cylinders tested under pressure in a vat of water to determine whether they should be discarded or taken on to the next production step. A Management by Exception System was designed, one that would plan and use the proper manpower to achieve a specific number of cylinders output each day. The supervisor consistently—and quite emotionally—maintained he would not do the planning system as outlined by the program. When management was finally called in, they found that the standard data sheet took the form of each isolated incident of the work flow, rather than a single flow unit itself. Therefore, the supervisor was being asked to plan how many cylinders he would lift, place into water, bring up under pressure, take down from pressure and enter into the flow. This, of course, was an example of the utter misuse of standard data. The supervisor became most cooperative once the data was changed to test cylinders and paint cylinders, and with the same manpower his output changed from 46 cylinders per day to near 200. Yet, this simple misunderstanding almost cost management a several hundred percent improvement in the operation through the use of the new system.

As it was, management straightened out the supervisor's misunderstanding which netted them an additional $3,369 profit per year from the same job.

METHODS OF CORRECTION

Once the standard data has been determined to be correct, and once the supervisor has gone on record that he was reviewed, worked with and can use that data, one of the surest methods of avoiding any supervisory misunderstandings is to have the supervisor explain to management how and why the system will be used. That explanation should include what methods he has available to him to prepare his plan, and how he can document his exceptions in such a manner that management will be brought into action when needed. Unless management is certain that the supervisor has a good working knowledge of not only the how's and why's of the system, but also of the standard data as well, no corrections will take place at a time of malfunction because no determination will have been made of the supervisor's comprehension of the system.

DISPLAYING THE RESULTS

Many times, management is remiss in publicizing the results of the system to all levels of the chain of command. They fail to inform the personnel functioning within the system of its results. Too often management discusses the system at their own level and never allows those subordinate levels to know that the system could not function without their wholehearted and continued participation. This can result in disaster, for those lower levels begin to believe that management is not using the facts passed on to them. It is incumbent upon management to publicize a system's results through graphs, bulletin board announcements, group meetings and awards, and to make it eminently clear to the subordinate levels that their problems are being attended to and will be solved, if identified. No system of Management by Exception can overcome the pitfalls of human frailty, unless management continues to demonstrate that the system's results are indeed being utilized, and that achievements have been made.

MANAGEMENT BY EXCEPTION POINTERS

1. The failure of a subordinate to implement his part of a Management by Exception System should in no way be the criterion for measuring either the validity of the plan or the system itself.
2. A manager must develop a system of cross checks *before* a system is committed to execution. One of the surest means of such cross checking is through the transposition of materials or work from one format to another.
3. When exceptions cease to be identified, the problem can almost invariably be traced to human frailty or negligence. On the other hand, when the system fails to produce results, it is very likely that the weakness can be found somewhere in the system itself.

4. Management must make it clear to all subordinate levels of the operation that a new system, however imperfect initially, will be given a fair test. Such endorsement encourages the pinpointing of weaknesses all along the line and aids in the modification and revision of the system.
5. Resistance to a new system will often take the form of overcompensation due to exaggerated reporting. Such resistance can best be overcome through the application of the several illustrative forms accompanying this chapter.
6. Audit forms generally fall into two broad categories: forms for the tally or documentation of statistics as they currently exist and forms that reflect volume or statistical data after it has been gathered. Both are essential for auditing an operation in such a way as to distinguish between human frailty and negligence and flaws in the system itself.
7. Management and systems designers must be absolutely certain that line supervisors understand those elements of an exception system pertinent to their operation. Such assurance comes best through requiring a supervisor to review the *totality* of the system, explaining its several elements.
8. Management should make an effort to involve all subordinate levels in the implementation and maintenance of an exception system by frequent reports on its results and achievements.

7

COST REDUCTION THROUGH MANAGEMENT BY EXCEPTION

"SO THE PLAN WAS BAD AFTER ALL . . . "

Many companies embark on large over-all planning systems which are founded in necessity and desire, more than hard basic fact and the ability to produce the end results. Because the final purpose of planning is an attempt to operate more effectively and/or profitably, and the desired result is an increase in productivity, sales and profit, the reasons for planning are sometimes obscured in the evaluation of the plan. Before one can evaluate exceptions to plans, it is ultimately necessary to evaluate the plan itself, its merit, its feasibility, its accuracy and the exceptions generated by a failure to execute the plan as designed. Some instrument, then, must be established to differentiate between a basically bad plan and a failure to consolidate or use exceptions. The difference between the two can be exceedingly fine, but it must be established by management in advance of performance of the plan. An example of this can be found when the necessity of price structuring available labor or competitive situations forces management into establishing a plan totally and absolutely beyond their capacity, abilities or current market positions.

To illustrate this point further, let's consider a company manufacturing space heaters and air conditioning units. This particular firm enjoyed about 12% of a regional market. Because of the increasing costs of labor and raw materials, as well as a steadily decreasing market place, this particular firm was forced to establish a budget plan which required a flat 20% increase in sales as well as a 20% improvement in productivity. As no new instrument of any kind had been introduced, save the necessity of an increased volume in productivity, this firm had, at the very offset, a plan that was initially bad. No revision was made during the course of the year in the initial planning. Valiant efforts were made by both the sales force and production group to achieve the goals established by the plan.

Upon conclusion of the year, the firm had increased its productivity by some 15% and achieved an improvement of around 10% in their sales figures. They had employed a partial Management by Exception system which allowed them to identify production problems, as well as problems generating lost sales. The achievements of this firm were markedly good. The ability to achieve the overall plan was not as good. In this case, it could be genuinely said that the plan itself was bad. Because the plan was bad, it completely clouded the positive results of increasing sales in the face of a declining market and improving productivity in the work force without new equipment or a new method or new personnel or new management. The improvements were good, the achievement of the total plan was not good. The plan itself had been bad, yet management had failed to recognize that. Had the top management of the firm plotted on a monthly basis the positive achievements in both sales and production, they would have come to grips with the hard fact that the plan itself was too overly ambitious to be achieved. They had, in essence, failed, and the second step where the pattern develops and the plan grows stronger never came into play.

A CASE IN POINT

One firm, as many, had grown from a one man operation to a 2,000 man company. In this case, the business was industrial construction. During the course of growth of this firm, the top man and his operating managers had always been capable of selling sufficient on-going-projects to keep the growth momentum of the company going forward.

Annually, the top group of managers had established a dollar goal for the company. They subtracted the cost of labor, materials and overhead to determine profit. As the firm grew, the profit diminished. As a recession moved in, the volume of projects also started to decline. The president looked to the systems people to come up with the solution. "The plan was bad after all . . ." The systems people quickly developed a standard data sheet for the president, which reflected the composite use of only 2-1/2 man years spent by all concerned on the sales element of the plan. True, in the past, each sales-man-month had generated a little over $1,000,000 worth of new sales. But, two things now entered into play. The first was a rapidly deteriorating market. Secondly, the firm called for a 25% increase in sales. When confronted with the initial sales-man-month requirements, the president recognized the first weakness in his plan: lack of sales-man-months. He hired new salesmen to first offset the lack of capacity and, secondly to offset the lack of market.

THE PATTERN DEVELOPS AND THE PLANS GROW STRONGER

When frequent plottings are made against any formal plan, the exceptions become more self evident. Therfore, in the cited case of the construction company, an annual sales plan had really only a single plotting made against the plan and could generate only a single exception. An expansion of the plan by incidents of feedback may be necessary to determine more than mere interim statistics. The purpose of more feedback with further detailing of the plan will afford the planner the ability to note the exceptions, which, in themselves, will start to establish a pattern.

Let's assume *all* plans are wrong. The initial problem the planner has is knowing where they are wrong. Because of this major assumption, the detailing and feedback mechanism must be both significant and within the realm of realistic plottings. Again looking at the construction sales, one will quickly recognize the inability to develop million dollar commitments on an hourly, daily or weekly basis. To detail a plan of sales efforts at the top management level would be almost counter-productive, as the established lead time to generate a sale is about three months. In this case, a quarterly plan would be possible, but a monthly plan would increase the ability of the management to watch the pattern develop. If the plan fails to materialize, new plans must be made. The form to accomplish this should not be complex. Figure 24 shows the method employed by the construction firm to plot the sales on a monthly basis when compared to the available consumption of sales-man-days. Here again, the top management plan would have to be detailed by the sales manager to reflect the markets, efforts and results of the months, as they applied to the salesmen. Figure 13 of Chapter 4 would now come into focus.

The plotting required for the president would be a yes or no, and the exception would be expressed in + or − dollars. This would only lead to questions pinpointing the reasons found at a lower level as to why the plotting is not going as planned.

As in the case of the construction firm, the deterioration of the market place reflected the necessity to cut overhead if the profit were to be maintained. This

Sales Dollar & Manpower Requirement Plan

ITEM											
		PLAN	ACTUAL	VARIANCE + −	PLAN	ACTUAL	VARIANCE + −	PLAN	ACTUAL	VARIANCE + −	PLAN
SALES	$ 1,000,000.										
	$ per Man Day										
	Man Day Req.										

FIGURE 24

Sales Dollar, Salesmen, Construction and Administration Plan

		JUNE			JULY			AUGUST		
		PLAN	ACTUAL	VARIANCE + −	PLAN	ACTUAL	VARIANCE + −	PLAN	ACTUAL	VARIANCE + −
SALES	$ 1,000,000	10								
	$ PER MAN DAY	125.00								
	MAN DAY REQ.	80								
OPERATIONS	BILLED $ (1,000,000)				.5			1.0		
	EARNED HOURS PER MILLION				23,000			23,000		
	EARNED HOURS REQUIRED				11,500			23,000		
ADMINIS										
EXEC	ADMINISTRATIVE HOURS PER DIRECT HOUR .30				3,450			6,900		
TOTAL CONSTRUCTION COMPANY										

FIGURE 25

plotting, in turn, generated the need for the identical method of planning, not only for the overhead, but also the construction management requirements as well. The expansion of the sales plan and the first three months' plotting developed the loss of the market. This directed the president to take a more detailed look at the other two elements of his operation, the accounting and clerical support and the construction crews. Figure 25 shows the addition to the overall plan and, when tied to some historical data developed by the systems people, reflects the lead times and effects of both ongoing projects as well as the entry of new sales. Thus, the president was allowed to plot the plus or minus effect of his sales plans against future requirements for accounting/clerical support as well as construction personnel demands.

This example was used effectively. While the firm took a decided loss in volume, the plotting of results, coupled with the re-planning and acting upon the information, afforded this firm a dramatic increase in profits.

Sales Dollar and Manpower Requirement Plan

								SIX MONTH TOTAL		
ACTUAL	VARIANCE + −	PLAN	ACTUAL	VARIANCE + −	PLAN	ACTUAL	VARIANCE + −	PLAN	ACTUAL	VARIANCE + −

FIGURE 24 (continued)

Sales Dollar, Salesmen, Construction and Administration Plan

SEPTEMBER			OCTOBER			NOVEMBER			SIX MONTH TOTAL		
PLAN	ACTUAL	VARIANCE + −	PLAN	ACTUAL	VARIANCE + −	PLAN	ACTUAL	VARIANCE + −	PLAN	ACTUAL	VARIANCE + −
1.0			1.5			2.0					
23,000			23,000			23,000					
23,000			34,500			46,000					
6,900			10,350			13,800					

FIGURE 25 (continued)

Too many times management does not look at the exceptions to their plans frequently enough. This results in the final and only knowledge coming at year's end, when the accountants close the books. Plans cannot be made stronger, unless management is willing to act on the exceptions and revise the plan as the exception directs.

Many times, such as in the construction case cited, the manager must look in the opposite direction for the adjustment to his initial plan when the pattern emerges. In this case, the former method of making profits was to subtract the established or anticipated costs of overhead as the method of establishing profit. Once the sales themselves were well planned within management's ability to act, the lump sum overhead figure didn't stand up. This firm dropped the overhead in direct proportion to the established demand created by sales. This was done after the actual impact of the demand was pre-determined in the expanded plan itself. Obviously, with ongoing projects and the delayed demand of new sales, one could not make a direct loss of sales reduction. When the relationship and mix of work was determined, the president was able to reduce his accounting/clerical work force accordingly. In this case, the work force was reduced from 50 employees to 15. This was unique to this firm, as they had never looked at the support areas as being directly related to sales. Yet, a quarter-million dollars of unneeded support was being employed because the top management had not worked out the ability to note where and when to make volume reductions.

IDENTIFY THE HIDDEN COSTS

Relationships to a function generally contain the major areas of hidden costs. When a Management Control by Exception System is set into place, these relationships will surface. The establishment of standard data used to plan, whether sales-man-months or cases per hour, will allow the exceptions to be noted. Hidden costs are almost always in the same categories as the simple stroke tallies of the exception groupings themselves. They are the "lack of" type and only lead management to the detailed identification of the problem. The solution to the problem is why management exists in the first place. As previously covered, the solution to one exception identified problem may create the identification of a heretofore hidden one.

A CASE IN POINT

A good example of this situation existed in the produce loading dock of a major metropolitan grocery chain. The hours of this operation ran from 1:00 A.M. until 9:30 A.M. In the early hours of the morning, the lettuce, eggs, oranges and various produce arrived by truck to be unloaded in the center of large open warehouses. By mid-morning checkers were allocating the various numbers of crates and boxes to the 10 sub-stations on the outside perimeters of the dock for re-loading into some 50 parked trailers, each pre-assigned to the various retail stores in the chain. The loaders at each sub-station would place the predetermined number of an item in each of the trucks assigned to their areas. A systems team had established standard data as to time requirements for the loading of, let's say, oranges from the center of the warehouse to the sub-stations, and from there to the trailers. In establishing this data, it was noted the checkers receiving the merchandise used a computer print-out to chalk the store number on each and every case received. These cases were, in turn, delivered to the substation where the loader would have the identical print-out for his stores, where he would sort the cases, place them in the trailer and check the entry on the print-out.

The systems men pointed out to the management the folly of establishing a specific case of oranges for sub-station #2, store #54, when the real requirement was for 178 cases at sub-station #2, where it didn't matter which of the cases went into which stores. Management concurred, and 7 people were let go at the checker station. Simple? Not unless you are looking for hidden costs. Further, the checkers were now able to load the trailers with nothing more than a gross count received. If, when the final trailer was being loaded, the remaining cases were long or short, a quick recount of the other loaded units could be made. The further hidden costs of over and under shipment with all the adjustments required also were reduced at the store level. Once this flow type de-bugging was accomplished, the mismatch of the volume demands were tackled. It had been identified that it required one man-hour for every 60 units of produce being handled. Initially, this unit of measure seemed to be only about half right, as the total units shipped each week were in the 60,000 range, yet the hours required were in the 2,000 hours per week range. Management took a closer look at the exceptions to the 60 unit hour plan and found on Mondays, Tuesdays and Wednesdays the performance dropped to lower than 30 units per man-hour. Yet, on Thursday and particularly Friday, the exception was far better than the expected 60 units per hour. Once these exceptions to the planned range were identified, a closer look at the volume and content of the volume was required. First, the volume was uneven. See Figure 26.

A quick look at the graph shows the labor force had to ship almost twice as many units of produce on Friday as they had on Tuesday. Yet, by the terms of the labor contract, work hours were for eight straight time hours per day, Monday through Friday, and no casual or part-time employees were allowed. Being unable to expand or contract the labor force, management was required to look elsewhere to level the work load. Customers at grocery stores can be moved to purchase perishable produce through price and specials to only a limited point, so changing the weekend buying habits of the customers offered only limited help. A simple stroke tally of all 50 retail stores ordering, plus a recognition of the difference between highly seasonal and regular items led to an interesting pattern, not too different from the Central File department in the large snack company. Figure 27 reflects the same volume under analysis between "soft" produce (lettuce, plums, etc.) and "hard" produce (apples, squash, potatoes). See Figure 27.

Here the retail stores were ordering the same amount of soft/hard produce each day. Not only were the retail stores causing the ups and downs demanded of a fixed work force, but also they were compounding the problem by ordering stock items during peak days. The riddle to the exceptions in performance was answered. This particular chain now orders hard produce in the first part of the week. This allows both the buyers, produce dock work force and the produce men in the retail stores to concentrate on the real problems caused by week-end customer demand and serve a higher grade merchandise. This warehouse now cycles produce units at 75 cases per man-hour with a much reduced labor force.

Uneven Product Volume Graph

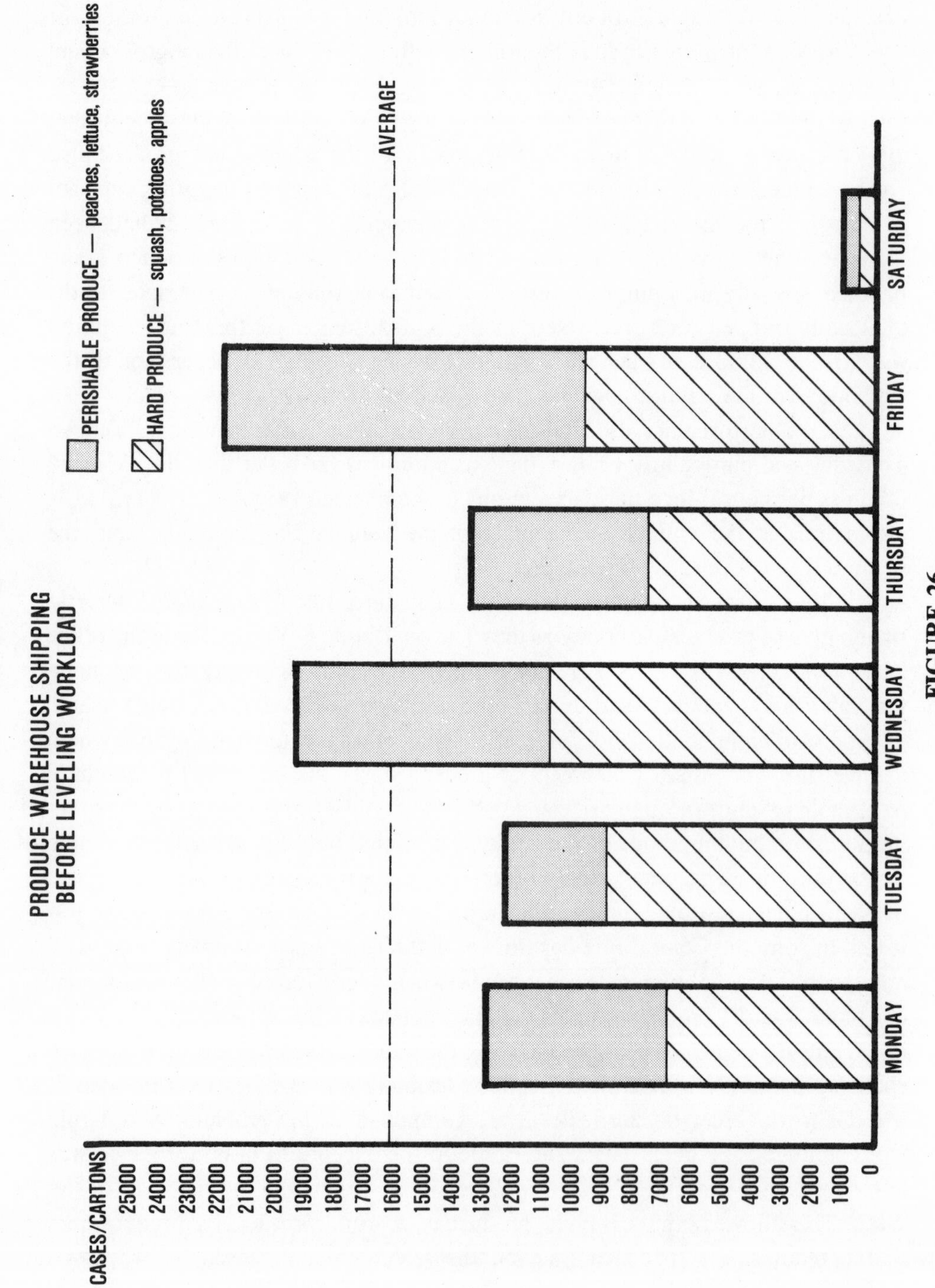

FIGURE 26

Level Produce Volume Graph

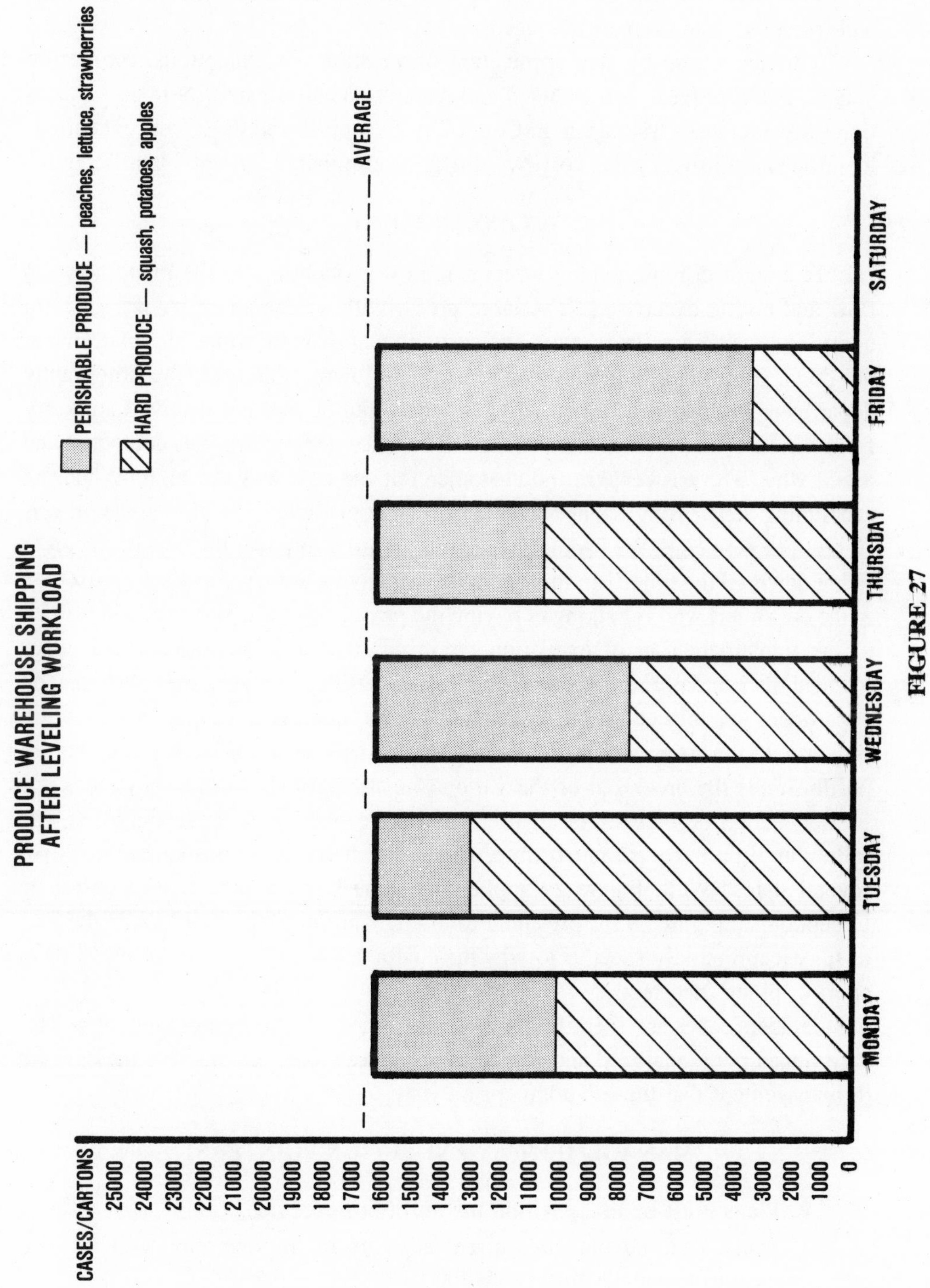

FIGURE 27

This reduction was over $200,000 in payroll at the end of the first year. Not bad for apples and oranges managed by exception.

Through a step by step application of working out exceptions, the performance was improved, cost reduced and frustrations eliminated. Now this operation truly operates a Management Control by Exception and those new exceptions identified are further hidden costs waiting to be eliminated through identification.

A CASE IN POINT

In a large printing plant a systems man was walking out the manufacturing flow and noting exceptions. The large press, with a 12 man crew, was idle. In querying the foreman as to why, the systems man was informed the plates were not down from the lithography department. Following this lead, the lithography department foreman was asked why. He answered he had not received authority from the customer for the plate change. The sales department was contacted and asked why. The answer was the customer felt the cost was too high. When the accounting department manager was asked why the quoted cost for a revision was so high, he replied, ''We had to change that in order to cover the cost of the press being down all the time!'' In this example, we have a hidden cost being passed on to the customer, who is balking at paying the price of an unsolved exception. Prior to the implementation of exception reporting, the decision makers had never realized the route of the costs and were losing business because of it. When each department was placed on the system, this same management saw this situation ring-around-the-rosey before them on a single sheet of paper each week. Figure 28 illustrates the break out of the various functions of the operation to look for further hidden problems. As all this was taking place in a single building, the follow-up didn't require much time. But, what if the areas are spread out over several states? Well, Figure 29 applies the same basic Management Control by Exception. In Figure 29 the president found the answer to the problem on the face of his exception tally sheet as to why his customers complained of being shipped short or billed incorrectly.

Hidden costs are identified by an exception to the completion of a predetermined plan, analyzed and solved. The stroke tallies are only the messengers to management that these hidden costs exist.

MANAGEMENT BY EXCEPTION POINTERS

1. Plans must be made within the ability to execute.
2. Plans made beyond the current capacity of the operation will succeed only if management expands the capacity.
3. Interrelationships between sales, manufacturing and support must be expanded proportionally if the initial plan calls for expansion.

Printing Plant Exception Report

— EXCEPTIONS —

SALES:

Item	Count
A. WAITING FOR PRODUCTION SCHEDULE	1
B. WAITING FOR PROOFS	
C. WAITING FOR ESTIMATES	12
D. LATE JOB DELIVERY	
E. JOBS INCORRECTLY SHIPPED	
F. INCORRECT INVOICING	
G. OTHER ____	

ADMINSTRATION:

Item	Count
AA. BAD CLOCK CARDS	6
BB. NO RECEIVING REPORT	
CC. NO MATERIAL ISSUE	9
DD. IMPROPERLY PREPARED RECEIVING SLIP	
EE. NO PURCHASE ORDER	
FF. OTHER ____	

PRODUCTION:

Item	Count
H. LACK OF VOLUME	10
I. LACK OF SPECIFICATION	
J. WAIT FOR PAPER OR INK	
K. JOB PRIORITY CHANGED	1
L. WAITING FOR PLATES	2
M. WAITING FOR LOCK-UP	
N. CUSTOMER DELAY	
O. CUSTOMER ALTERATION	
P. WAITING FOR PRODUCTION SCHEDULE	
Q. EMPLOYEE TRAINING REQUIRED	6
R. MECHANICAL PROBLEMS	
S. MAINTENANCE	1
T. POOR LAYOUT	
U. BAD SIGNATURES	
V. PAPER PROBLEMS	8
W. OTHER ____	
X. OTHER ____	

FIGURE 28

Cross Discipline Exception Report

— EXCEPTIONS —

PLANTS

	S. OHIO	N. OHIO	GEORGIA	N. FLORIDA	S. FLORIDA
MACHINE BREAKDOWN					
LACK OF MATERIALS					
REWASH					
OTHER					

SALES / SERVICE

	S. OHIO	N. OHIO	GEORGIA	N. FLORIDA	S. FLORIDA
INCORRECT INVOICES					
EQUIPMENT BREAKDOWN					
SHORTAGES					
ACCOUNT QUITS - NUMBER					
ACCOUNT QUITS - DOLLARS					
NEW ACCOUNTS - NUMBER					
NEW ACCOUNTS - DOLLARS					
ROUTE DELIVERY PROBLEMS					
OTHER					

OFFICE

	S. OHIO	N. OHIO	GEORGIA	N. FLORIDA	S. FLORIDA
POOR INFORMATION FROM SALES					
WAIT FOR DATA PROCESSING					
CAN'T MATCH PAYMENT/INVOICE					
WAIT INFO OUTLYING AREAS					
CUSTOMER COMPLAINTS					
OTHER					

FIGURE 29

4. Various areas of an operation do not necessarily require expansion in the same time period.
5. Irregular input demand may direct unnecessary expansion to accommodate the failure to plan a level input.
6. Planning at executive level requires information from all areas within the same period of time.
7. Problems in one part of an operation may be solved by identifying exceptions in another area.

8

MANAGEMENT BY EXCEPTION FOR THE CONSTRUCTION INDUSTRY

A REVIEW OF CONSTRUCTION METHODS

Perhaps no single industry suffers as much from a lack of Management by Exception as the construction industry. Yet, ironically, by the very nature of this industry, they have more material in advance than most to lay out a complete system of Management by Exception.

A review of construction methods is in order. First, regardless of the methods of disciplines to be employed in construction, the estimate or bid starts the whole chain of events which will eventually lead to the completed project. From the most modest home to a massive hydro-electric dam and waterway project and all the myriad of projects between these two extremes, an estimate or bid initiates the project. True, in many cases the blueprints, or, as the systems man would recognize them, plans are not extant at the time of the initial estimate or bid. The absence of prints in no way stops an estimate or bid being given, for most contractors use their past experience to formulate a ''square foot' or ''lineal foot'' estimate subject to final prints. While this method can be sound, it currently gives vent to spiraling costs. The absence of a simple Management by Exception system, found so often in contracting, means the gross cost of the former projects already contains the errors and overruns of close management control. From this initial fallacy evolves the unpleasant surprises of bad estimates which have plagued the industry for so long. The high incidence of contractors going broke or buyers having to pay 25% to 50% more for a project completed two to five months late finds its roots in this method of long division, utilizing past projects to determine the cost of the proposed one.

Notwithstanding an error in the "square foot" bid, eventually, the project will have to be finished with detailed plans (blueprints) completed. Here again, the contractor may avoid the tools available to firmly establish a Management by Exception system. The more detailed the prints, the more control is afforded the contractor, yet almost never does the contractor translate the prints into the raw aid data used to formulate a time-cost frame system of Management by Exception.

CASE IN POINT

A medium size home builder in the Western United States operated from a specific set of prints for all the home models he constructed. He prided himself on giving his buyers homes which were not tract models, but custom-made to their own specifications. True, they were evolved from base type units and modified from that point. Yet, this contractor never took the time to establish the base cost and build-up the change costs. He relied instead on his "square foot" cost of the past completed homes. Therefore, if a client looked at a split level of 1,350 square feet and modified the plans to 1,400 square feet, the contractor would compute the square footage cost of the last 1,400 square foot home and multiply out the proposed cost. He arrived at the feeling that something was missing, when each year his accountants showed his net profit before taxes was less than half the amount he was adding into the projects. As this contractor was working on a fixed cost basis, he had to absorb all errors. A systems man was called in to rectify the problem of the missing profits. The solution was easy to identify. A look at the original bid build-up had lumped all the cost factors together, the sheetrock, siding, 2 x 4's, etc. No specific take-off of the modified prints was being made. A phase sheet coming directly from a take-off of the final prints was introduced, and the seepage through oversight was corrected.

THE FIRST STEP TO THE ESTABLISHMENT OF A MANAGEMENT BY EXCEPTION SYSTEM IN CONSTRUCTION

Using the prints as aids to formulate the phases of the home construction, the systems man was able to identify the correct amount of 2 x 4's, plywood, etc., not only as it applied to the total bill of materials, but also as its consumption was required as the home was built. Figure 30 reflects the original method of estimating. The original method of estimating laid out the basic steps used in the construction of a house. After the initial entries an entry such as the "all building material, lumber or, mill work, etc." is found. Here is only a one-step refinement of the "square-foot" method once again. True, the estimate pulls much of the cost into separate categories, but for 100% of the material entry, the only exception would be right or wrong, and then only upon completion of the house. This is much too broad a lumping to be safe, and it is all but useless in a system of Management by Exception.

In order to correct the estimate and lay it out in a manner usable for a Management by Exception System, it is necessary to truly lay out the entries in precedence. On the original sheet "plumbing," for instance, appears well down the list as a total category. Yet, a closer examination of the time related method of building the house would indicate all the rough-in work for plumbing, electric, heating and air conditioning must be done simultaneously with the framing and bracing phase, which is one of the first steps in the erection of the house. Yet, the final fixtures in plumbing are completed as one of the final steps of construction. While the entry of "plumbing" appears to be one, it isn't. The commitment of materials, labor and equipment plus the inter-relationship of different crafts, in this case, carpentry, requires more than one entry for "plumbing." Once the time-phased inter-relationship of the construction has been developed, the preparation of an estimate is usable not only for predicting the cost of labor and materials with a reasonable degree of certainty, but also for other plans as well. If the same estimate sheet, as shown in Figure 30, is laid out in order of precedence, as illustrated in Figure 31, the basis for Management by Exception is well established. By estimating in the same manner as the work is to be completed, a time related check list has been made. If no further use of Management by Exception was to be made, the off schedule or exception aspect of the project would appear through the use of a simple check off weekly of the estimate. If the project is straight line and simple, that method would suffice. Most construction, however, is much more complex and requires more set-up work. Labor may be scheduled hourly, by the phase or by the piece. Some work may be performed by a third party on a fixed basis. So, an expansion of the Estimate Worksheet should be made. Figure 32 shows the same basic information as Figure 31. Here, however, an expansion is made to accommodate the other requirements of setting up a costing and control system of Management by Exception. Note the addition of a cost code on the left. The first number indicates a phase in building a house; the second number is a step required to complete the phase. The phases become time and dollar check points. If ahead or behind, they identify the exceptions in time to avoid excess costs and time requirements. The other additions are made to insure that complete labor and material cost is being considered, regardless of the method employed to accomplish the work. Once completed, the manager has a one sheet visual layout of his total costs by phase, steps, method of completion and dollars. If his profit fails to materialize as planned, he can pinpoint the exceptions to his estimate on his next one, rather than accept and include it. His old estimate becomes an aid for his newest one.

ORIGINAL BID ESTIMATE SHEET

		Estimated Cost
Appraisal or FHA Commitment Fee		
Survey, Blueprints & Permits		
Excavating, Rough Grading and Backfill	LABOR	
	MATERIAL	
Topsoil, Sod Finish Grade, Seed, Trees & Shrubs	LABOR	
	MATERIAL	
Foundations and Footings	LABOR	
	MATERIAL	
Damp proof, Drain Tile and Termite Shield	LABOR	
	MATERIAL	
Bsmt Floor, Steps and/or Walks	LABOR	
	MATERIAL	
Chimney-Fireplace Veneer	LABOR	
	MATERIAL	
Driveway: Concrete Blacktop Crushed Rock (Ck. One)	LABOR	
	MATERIAL	
All Building Material Lumber, Millwork, etc.		
Cabinets-Countertops	LABOR	
	MATERIAL	
Built-in Appliances (oven, cooktop-hood)	LABOR	
	MATERIAL	
Free Standing Appliances		
Carpenter Labor		
Floor Sanding and Finishing	LABOR	
	MATERIAL	
Floor Tile Carpet Roll Goods	LABOR	
	MATERIAL	
Wall Tile	LABOR	
	MATERIAL	
Gutters and Down Spouts	LABOR	
	MATERIAL	
Medicine Cabinet and Mirror	LABOR	
	MATERIAL	

FIGURE 30

Plastering	LABOR	
	MATERIAL	
Sheetrock Taping and Sanding	LABOR	
	MATERIAL	
Painting and Decorating	LABOR	
	MATERIAL	
Electrical	LABOR	
including $ Fixture Allow.	MATERIAL	
Sewer Stub in Gas and Water	LABOR	
Hook up	MATERIAL	
Plumbing	LABOR	
	MATERIAL	
Heating-Cooling	LABOR	
	MATERIAL	
Miscellaneous Loan Expense Rev.	LABOR	
Stamps, Heat, Electricity, etc.	MATERIAL	
SUB TOTAL		
Insurance		
%Overhead and Profit		
Loan Discount		
Interest on Construction Loan		
Sales Commission		
Building Site		
Total		

FIGURE 30 (continued)

BID ESTIMATE SHEET IN SEQUENCE

Item Description	Estimate Cost
Lot Price Survey, Blueprints, Permits Insurance—Builders, Risk HOW Premium	
Excavation Sewer, Water, Stub-in Back Fill, Rough Grading Electrical Trenching Electric Hook-up	
Footings Foundation Damp Proof Basement Floor Garage Floor Walks & Stoops Driveways	

FIGURE 31

Patios, Ret. Walls, Terraces	
Framing, Bracing, 1st Floor, Wall Sys	
Framing, 2nd Floor & Wall System	
Framing Roof System	
Fireplace, Chimney	
Framing Exterior Doors & Windows	
Framing Exterior Siding	
Decks	
Plumbing Rough	
Heating, Air Conditioning Rough	
Electrical Rough	
Telephone Rough	
Gas Line Hook-up	
Roofing	
Gutters & Down Spouts	
Insulation	
Dry Wall—Hanging	
Dry Wall Tape & Texture	
Veneer—Interior & Exterior	
Painting—Exterior	
Painting—Interior	
Interior Trim	
Cabinets—Counters	
Built-in Applicances	
Floor Covering	
Medicine Cabinet-Mirror-Bath Acc.	
Electric Fixtures	
Plumbing Fixtures	
Heating, Air Conditioning Finish	
Landscaping	
Post, Light, Mailbox	
Detail—Clean-up	
Detail—Final Adjustments	
Detail—Call Backs	
Loan Discount	
Interest on Construction Loan	
Sales Expense	
R.E. Taxes, Title Ins., Appraisal Fee	
Misc.—Utility Costs, Interest, Etc.	
Overhead—Fixed & Variable	
Sub-Total	
Total Price	
Profit	

FIGURE 31 (continued)

Expanded Bid Estimate Sheet

Cost Code		Item Description	Total Labor $	Total Material $	Estimate Cost
1	1	Lot Price			
1	2	Survey, Blueprints, Permits			
1	3	Insurance—Builders, Risk			
1	4	HOW Premium			
2	1	Excavation			
2	2	Sewer, Water, Stub-in			
2	3	Back Fill, Rough Grading			
2	4	Electrical Trenching			
2	5	Electric Hook-up			
3	1	Footings			
3	2	Foundation			
3	3	Damp Proof			
3	4	Basement Floor			
3	5	Garage Floor			
3	6	Walks & Stoops			
3	7	Driveways			
3	8	Patios, Ret. Walls, Terrace			
4	1	Framing, Bracing, 1st Floor, Wall Sys			
4	2	Framing, 2nd Floor & Wall System			
4	3	Framing Roof System			
4	4	Fireplace, Chimney			
4	5	Framing Exterior Doors & Windows			
4	6	Framing Exterior Siding			
4	7	Decks			
5	1	Plumbing Rough			
5	2	Heating, Air Conditioning Rough			
5	3	Electrical Rough			
5	4	Telephone Rough			
5	5	Gase Line Hook-up			
6	1	Roofing			
6	2	Gutters & Down Spouts			
7	1	Insulation			
7	2	Dry Wall—Hanging			
7	3	Dry Wall Tape & Texture			
7	4	Veneer—Interior & Exterior			
8	1	Painting—Exterior			
8	2	Painting—Interior			
8	3	Interior Trim			
8	4	Cabinets—Counters			
9	1	Built-in Appliances			
9	3	Floor Covering			

FIGURE 32

Cost Code		Item Description	Total Labor $	Total Material $	Estimate Cost
9	4	Medicine Cabinet-Mirror-Bath Acc.			
9	5	Electric Fixtures			
9	6	Plumbing Fixtures			
9	7	Heating, Air Conditioning Finish			
9	8	Landscaping			
9	9	Post, Light, Mailbox			
10	1	Detail—Clean-up			
10	2	Detail—Final Adjustments			
10	3	Detail—Call Backs			
10	4	Loan Discount			
10	5	Interest on Construction Loan			
10	6	Sales Expense			
10	7	R.E. Taxes, Title Ins., Appraisal Fee			
10	8	Misc.—Utility Costs, Interest, Etc.			
10	9	Overhead—Fixed & Variable			
SUB-TOTAL					
TOTAL PRICE					
PROFIT					

FIGURE 32 (continued)

One large construction firm found it was being awarded only 3% of the total estimate bids made. When a systems man suggested to the president of that firm that he should re-estimate the last bid made and lost in order to review why, the advice fell on deaf ears. Once this same firm had a phase estimate laid out, this same president re-estimates all lost bids at the executive level. This firm now is awarded over 60% of all bids made. The company has learned the value of popping up the exceptions with a pencil instead of their profit.

The use of the corrected method of estimating will help resolve the mystery of the lost profit. This new method enabled to contractor to establish his true cost of constructing the home prior to a firm commitment to the buyer. Those custom changes were not always in proportion to the addition of square footage, and so this contractor now had established his workable plan so necessary in a Management by Exception System.

While the above case in point may be simple, the elements of profit loss are the same if one jumps from the local home builder to one of the giants in the industrial construction industry. The local home builder's problem with five to ten blueprints jumps now from 5,000 to 10,000 detailed prints of the most complex variety. Yet, the same problem arises. The Exotic Chemical Company wants a bid on a $50,000,000 petro-chemical plant, but their final prints haven't been completed yet, nor will they be completed until the project is well under way. Therefore, Exotic Chemical will accept a cost plus fixed fee bid. How is the initial bid compiled—you know it—long division over the past similar projects, with all the mistakes and errors computed into the "square foot" estimate. The only change taking place is the magnitude of the numbers. The home builder quoted $43 a square foot. The giant industrial contractor quoted $430—the same method, the same lack of Management by Exception rules.

A CASE IN POINT

A large industrial contracting firm in the Southeast bid a multi-million dollar industrial plant on the "square footage" cost plus fixed fee method—detailed prints to follow during the course of the project. No matter how much manpower was placed on the project to control the costs by both the contractor and the client, those costs started to creep up by the millions. All the added controls and personnel were too late. Time was not allocated to nail down the real costs of the prints before they entered construction. A large staff was formulated to establish the cost, as in many cases, after the construction had been completed.

Coupled with this lack of establishing a plan, came the rapid increase in the cost of materials. Costs skyrocketed, and the completion dates kept creeping further and further into the future. The client and contractor both ended up very unhappy with weekly crisis meetings, which were well steeped in accompanying memos to each other. This contractor vowed "never again" and called in a systems firm. The first step toward establishing a Management by Exception System was to standardize the estimating system, regardless of the submission of the prints. Heretofore, the estimating department had been employed as a step prior to a sale. Estimates were varied in build-up and standard data being prepared. In fact, no two estimates were prepared in the same manner, and past projects information was relied upon for the "square foot" rules. Certainly a most invalid unit of measure in the days when construction materials can double in price during the course of the prior project.

The same method of detailed estimate build-up was instituted, whereby management could start with a firm plan. Figure 33 reflects the same basic method of detailed build-up of the labor/material cost components. Discipline was maintained on the estimators to follow the same logic and format, which enabled management to review the plan before entering the execution stage. Further, more detailed prints were submitted during the course of the project and were built up in the identical manner. This first step enabled the largest and most costly exceptions to be identified in advance. Because the initial emphasis was placed at the initial planning phase, cost exceptions and completion time changes were known very shortly after submission. Once implemented, this construction firm was able to convince the client of the value of continuing a detailed estimate prior to construc-

Detailed Estimate Worksheet

LINE	COST CODE	ITEM DESCRIPTION	UNIT OF MEASURE	VOLUME	LABOR			
					CREW NUMBER	PRODUC-TIVITY INDEX	MANPOWER PER UNIT	TOTAL MANHOURS
1								
2								
3								
4								
5								
6								
7								
8								
9								
10								
11								
12								
13								
14								
15								
16								
17								
18								
19								
20								
21								
22								
23								
24								
25								
26								
27								
28								
29								
30								
31								
32								
33								
34								
	TOTAL							

FIGURE 33

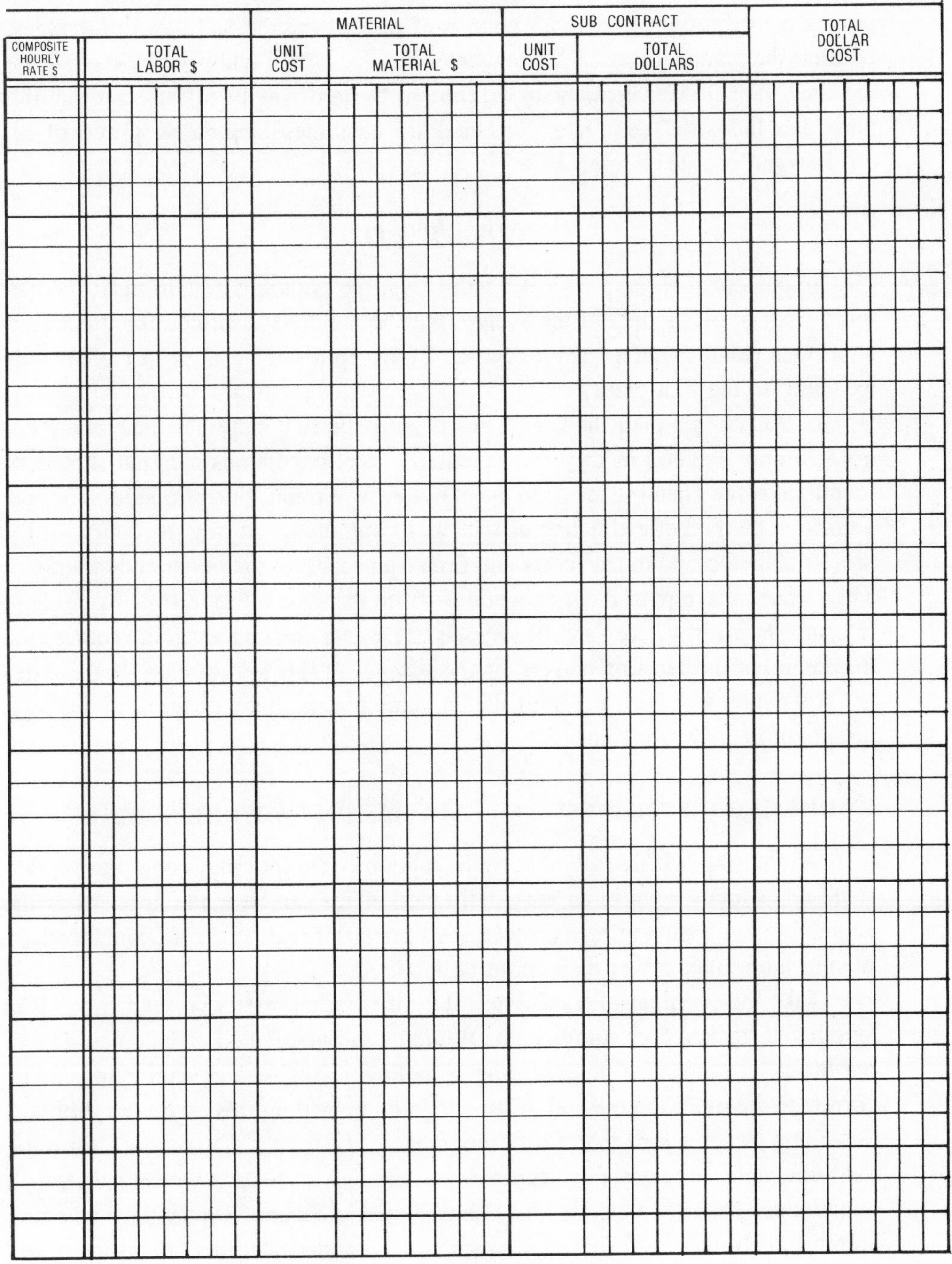

		MATERIAL		SUB CONTRACT		TOTAL DOLLAR COST
COMPOSITE HOURLY RATE $	TOTAL LABOR $	UNIT COST	TOTAL MATERIAL $	UNIT COST	TOTAL DOLLARS	

FIGURE 33

tion. Projects are now being completed within the time frame and cost as agreed to by both parties. This is a far cry from the prior chemical plant, where a data processing print-out of some 25 pounds of paper bore the bad news each week, because the planning step of Manangement by Exception had been by-passed. By the time the full Management by Exception System was in full use a year, this particular industrial contractor was making headlines nationally, proud of his on-time and cost performance.

ESTABLISH A PLAN

In construction as in all other industries, the planning system must be mastered first, or all the rest of the system will be lamely substituted for its ommission. One cannot manage any endeavor by exception if no norm (or plan) is in existence in the first place.

Establishing a plan, however, is still only the first step. The best laid plans are still only as good as they are executed. True, exceptions can and should be identified at the planning level. In the above case in point, the introduction of both a uniform method of estimating as well as a continuance during the course of the project helped pinpoint true costs and time frames. Both the buyer and contractor were, once in receipt of these exceptions (from the square foot estimates), able to re-establish priority, cost and time goals. The decision, once again, comes into the control of the decision makers. In the absence of this information, both parties are at the mercy of facts accomplished and are placed in the position of reacting, instead of decision making.

DETAILING ESTIMATES AND ESTABLISHING A WORK SCHEDULE

As the rules of Management by Exception come into play, one must understand no estimate done in an air-conditioned office can be made in terms of the actual format on site during a project. As a matter of fact, to do so would initially require more man-power than could be justified.

Take the example of a mechanical configuration stretching half a block in length and stacked four stories high. While an initial detailed estimate could call out the exact number of pipes, fitting, couplings, gauges, and such items and be correct in the total, the method of working and managing this aspect might break down into pieces and parts in a different manner. Like the ''square foot'' formula, the total might be reasonably accurate, and the only exception would occur upon completion. Detailed estimates such as reflected in Figure 33 must have a second step taken. In the first estimating example of the home builder, the priority and phases were merged into a single sheet. From the home builder's estimate all the project manager would have to do is take the estimate to a work schedule. This is simple enough, due to the relative familiarity of the work and easy phases. At the project manager's level the cost of insurance, titles, overhead and taxes is not his concern.

A relatively simple modification of Figure 31 becomes a job schedule for the house. The addition of the time frame across the top allows the manager to rework the estimate into his own time frame or plan. Figure 34 reflects a simple house schedule laid out by day through the use of a Ghant graph method. The overlaps and jam-ups are quickly evident. This method allows the controlling of subcontractors, independent carpenters, brick layers and the like. Further, when lulls or bottlenecks are noted, the schedule from other houses can be used to keep the workmen occupied when they would otherwise be idle through lack of management knowledge. The simple Ghant graph schedule still leaves the basic element of exception identification open, however. Figure 34 can and should be opened up to look like Figure 35. Here, the various crafts—subcontractors, piece workers and hourly employees—can be assigned to enter the actual completion line. This now allows the manager, foreman and home buyer a visual ability to watch the progress of the home on a day to day basis. It also acts as a strong visual highlight to exceptions and their management. Once again, where the construction is simple and straight-lined, Figure 35 will do quite well. Not so, in complex or unique projects. Here, an interim step must be taken to break down the thousands of parts into similar work controlled groups. In order to accomplish this step, the use of a computer and cost codes can be used to bypass the need for clerical re-stacking. But whether this is accomplished manually or through data processing, the end result is the same. A construction or work schedule must be accomplished. The achievement of the Work Schedule triggers the second major Management by Exception control.

A detailed estimate can call for some seemingly impossible tasks when spread against a work schedule. As an example, all the cranes are required at the same time, or 650 men one week and 200 the following. These examples reflect impossible demands caused by a failure to plan and are valid exceptions which, without the detailed estimate being broken down in advance, are being attempted today in many construction projects. The cost reflects the result in an exception of over-run costs. One of the easiest manners of detecting this exception is to find large numbers of equipment or men idle on a project, or stacks or materials gethering dust for long periods of time.

Figure 36 shows a method of re-stacking the detailed estimate into a work schedule, listing the activities only. This form reflects the theory of allowing early start and late start dates for the incremental steps of the project, to offset the lack of realistic manpower and material jam-ups. While this phase of establishing a Management by Exception System is dependent on a detailed estimate, it can be

Construction Job Schedule

CONSTRUCTION JOB SCHEDULE

		1st					2nd					3rd					4th					5th					6th		
PHASE STEPS		M	T	W	TH	F	M	T	W	TH	F	M	T	W	TH	F	M	T	W	TH	F	M	T	W	TH	F	M	T	W
		5/3	5/4	5/5	5/6	5/7	5/10	5/11	5/12	5/13	5/14	5/17	5/18	5/19	5/20	5/21	5/24	5/25	5/26	5/27	5/28	5/31	6/1	6/2	6/3	6/4	6/7	6/8	6/9
SURVEY, BLPRT, PERMIT	1-0																												
EXCAVATION	2-1																												
STUB-IN	2-2																												
BACK FILL, GRADING	2-3																												
TRENCHING	2-4																												
HOOK-UP	2-5																												
FOOTINGS	3-1																												
FOUNDATION	3-2																												
DAMP PROOF	3-3																												
BASEMENT-GARAGE FL.	3-4																												
WALKS, DRIVE, PATIO, ST.	3-6																												
FRAMING, BRACING 1st	4-1																												
FRAMING 2nd FLOOR	4-2																												
FRAMING ROOF SYSTEM	4-3																												
FRAMING EXTR. TRIM	4-4																												
FRAMING EXTR. WALL	4-5																												
DECKS	4-6																					MEMORIAL DAY							
PLUMBING ROUGH MTLS.	5-1																												
HTG, AIR CON. ROUGH	5-2																												
ELECTRICAL ROUGH MTL.	5-3																												
TELEPHONE ROUGH	5-4																												
ROOFING-GUTTERS	6-1																												
INSULATION	7-1																												
DRY WALL - HANG - TAPE	7-2																												
CHIMNEY, FIREPL. VEN.	7-4																												
PAINTING-EXTR-INTR.	8-1																												
CAB-MED CAB-COUNTER	9-1																												
BUILT-IN APPLIANCE	9-2																												
FREE STANDING APPL.	9-3																												
FLOOR COVERING	9-4																												
ELEC. FIXTURE-LAB-MTR.	9-6																												
PLBG. FIXTURE-LAB-MTR.	9-7																												
HTG. AIR CON-LAB-MTRL.	9-8																												
POST, LIGHT, MAILBOX	9-9																												
CLEAN-UP FINAL ADJ.	10-1																												

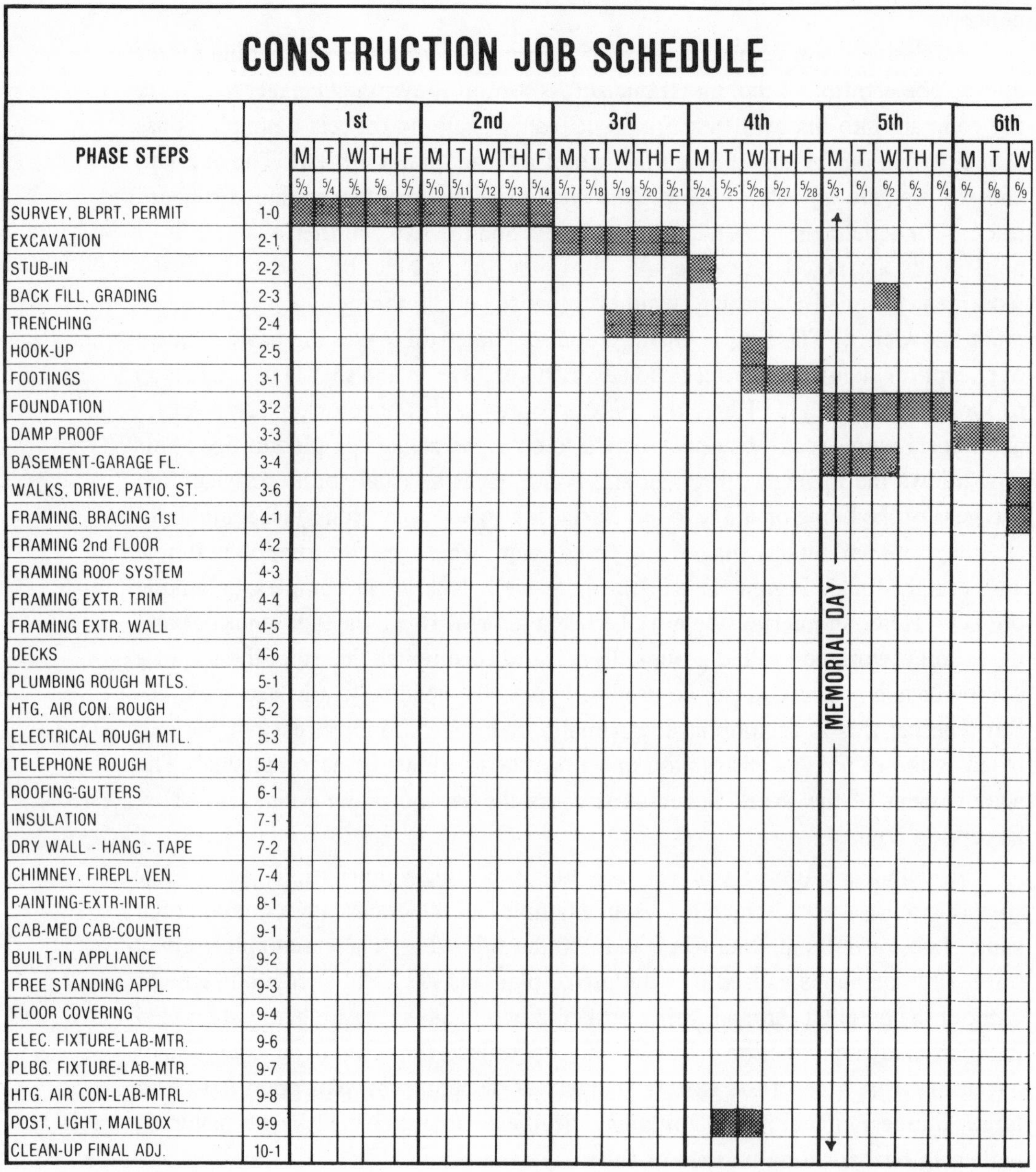

FIGURE 34

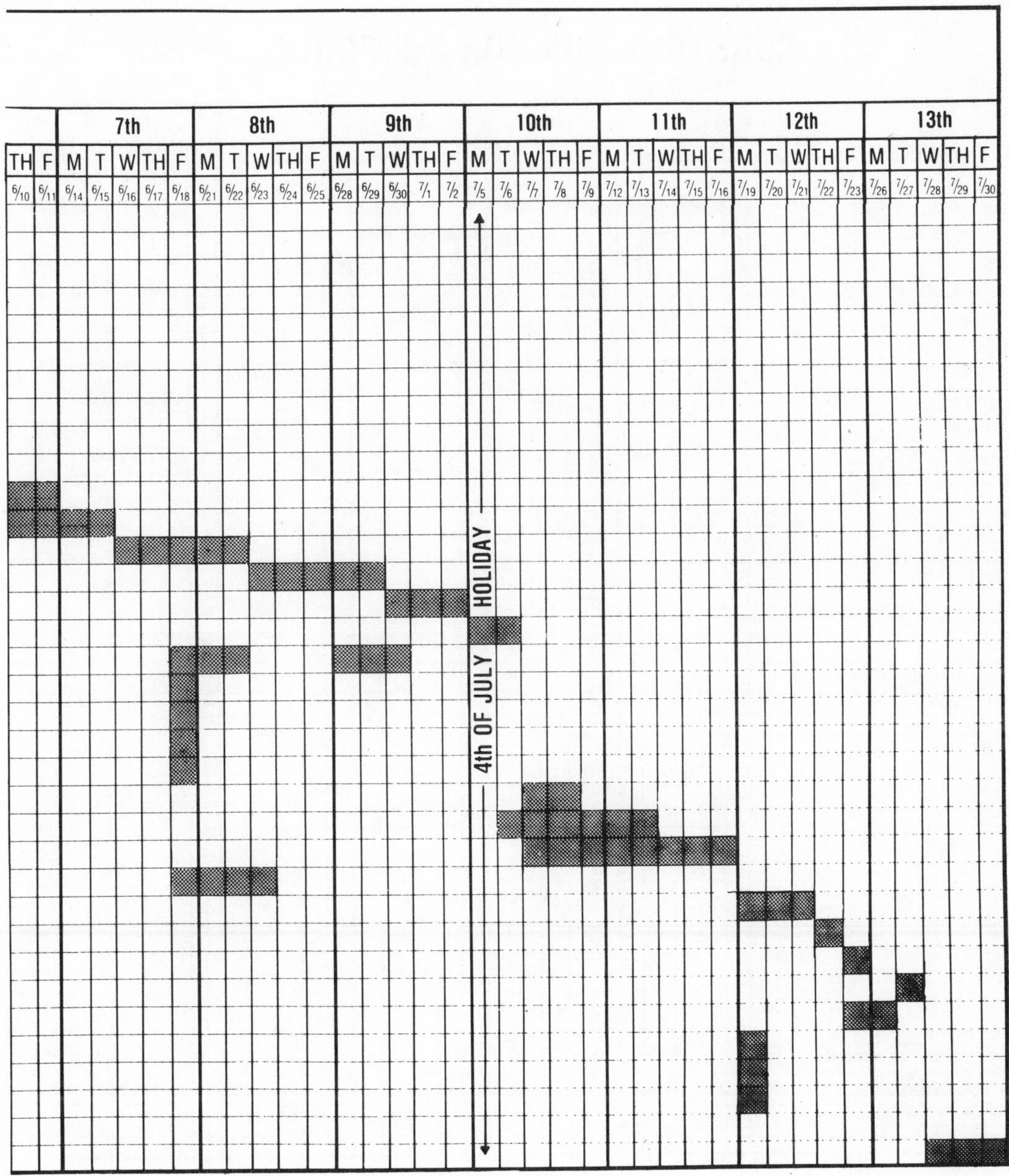
7th
8th
9th
10th
11th
12th
13th
TH F M T W TH F M T W TH F M T W TH F M T W TH F M T W TH F M T W TH F M T W TH F
6/10 6/11 6/14 6/15 6/16 6/17 6/18 6/21 6/22 6/23 6/24 6/25 6/28 6/29 6/30 7/1 7/2 7/5 7/6 7/7 7/8 7/9 7/12 7/13 7/14 7/15 7/16 7/19 7/20 7/21 7/22 7/23 7/26 7/27 7/28 7/29 7/30
4th OF JULY HOLIDAY

Construction Job Schedule with Exceptions Noted

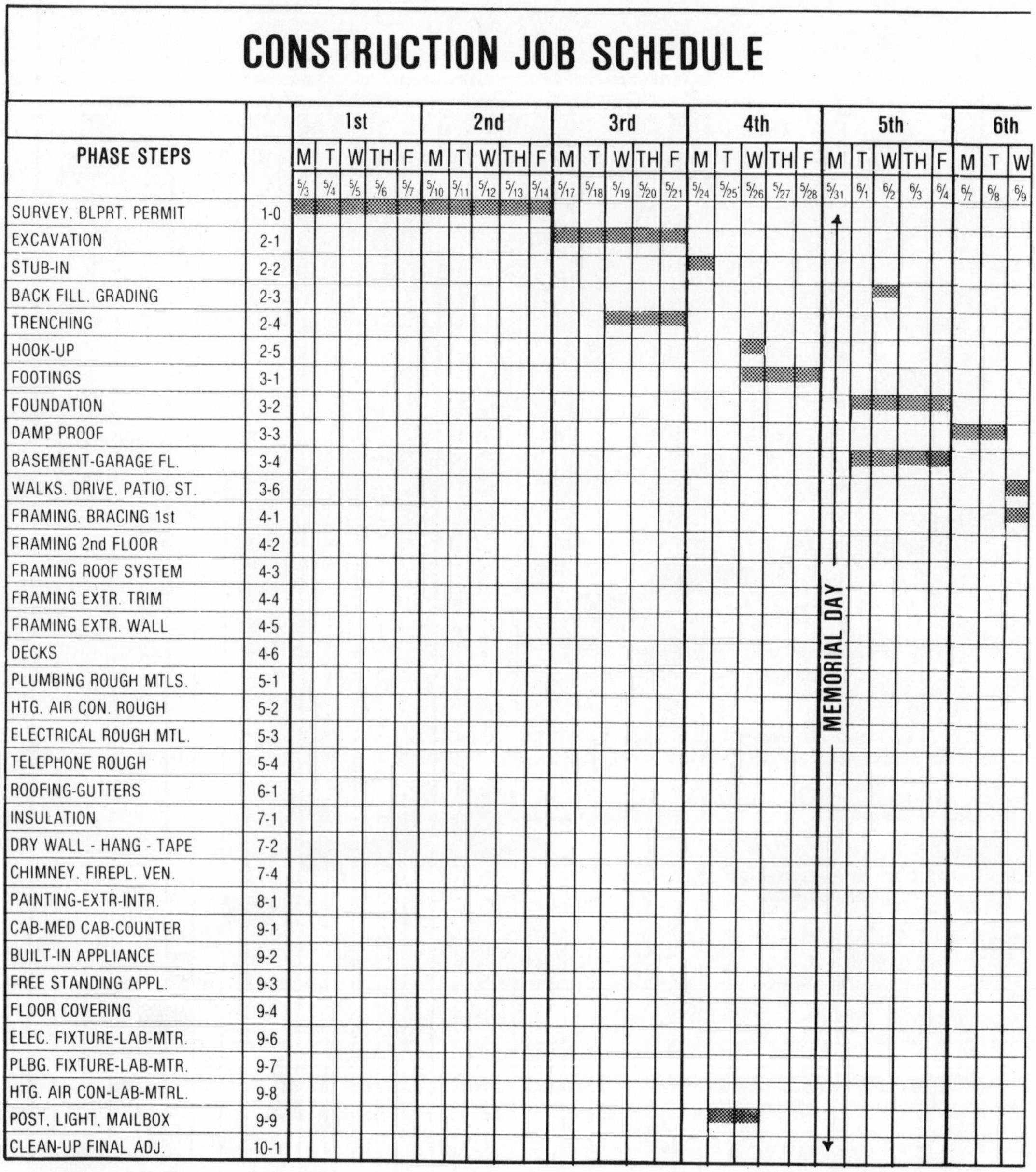

CONSTRUCTION JOB SCHEDULE

		1st					2nd					3rd					4th					5th					6th		
PHASE STEPS		M	T	W	TH	F	M	T	W	TH	F	M	T	W	TH	F	M	T	W	TH	F	M	T	W	TH	F	M	T	W
		5/3	5/4	5/5	5/6	5/7	5/10	5/11	5/12	5/13	5/14	5/17	5/18	5/19	5/20	5/21	5/24	5/25	5/26	5/27	5/28	5/31	6/1	6/2	6/3	6/4	6/7	6/8	6/9
SURVEY. BLPRT. PERMIT	1-0																												
EXCAVATION	2-1																												
STUB-IN	2-2																												
BACK FILL. GRADING	2-3																												
TRENCHING	2-4																												
HOOK-UP	2-5																												
FOOTINGS	3-1																												
FOUNDATION	3-2																												
DAMP PROOF	3-3																												
BASEMENT-GARAGE FL.	3-4																												
WALKS. DRIVE. PATIO. ST.	3-6																												
FRAMING. BRACING 1st	4-1																												
FRAMING 2nd FLOOR	4-2																												
FRAMING ROOF SYSTEM	4-3																												
FRAMING EXTR. TRIM	4-4																												
FRAMING EXTR. WALL	4-5																					MEMORIAL DAY							
DECKS	4-6																												
PLUMBING ROUGH MTLS.	5-1																												
HTG. AIR CON. ROUGH	5-2																												
ELECTRICAL ROUGH MTL.	5-3																												
TELEPHONE ROUGH	5-4																												
ROOFING-GUTTERS	6-1																												
INSULATION	7-1																												
DRY WALL - HANG - TAPE	7-2																												
CHIMNEY. FIREPL. VEN.	7-4																												
PAINTING-EXTR-INTR.	8-1																												
CAB-MED CAB-COUNTER	9-1																												
BUILT-IN APPLIANCE	9-2																												
FREE STANDING APPL.	9-3																												
FLOOR COVERING	9-4																												
ELEC. FIXTURE-LAB-MTR.	9-6																												
PLBG. FIXTURE-LAB-MTR.	9-7																												
HTG. AIR CON-LAB-MTRL.	9-8																												
POST. LIGHT. MAILBOX	9-9																												
CLEAN-UP FINAL ADJ.	10-1																												

FIGURE 35

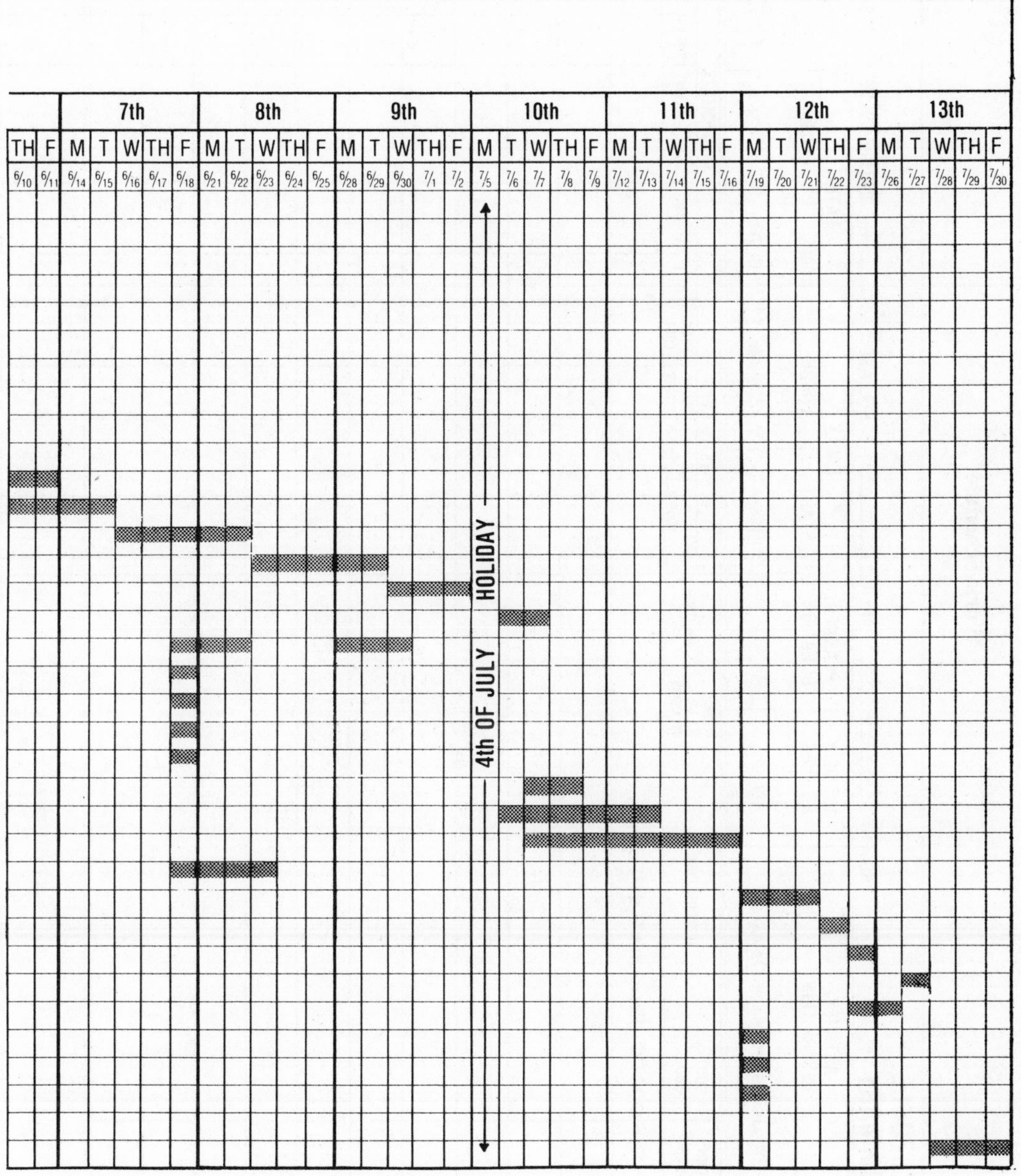
7th
8th
9th
10th
11th
12th
13th
TH F M T W TH F M T W TH F M T W TH F M T W TH F M T W TH F M T W TH F M T W TH F
6/10 6/11 6/14 6/15 6/16 6/17 6/18 6/21 6/22 6/23 6/24 6/25 6/28 6/29 6/30 7/1 7/2 7/5 7/6 7/7 7/8 7/9 7/12 7/13 7/14 7/15 7/16 7/19 7/20 7/21 7/22 7/23 7/26 7/27 7/28 7/29 7/30
4th OF JULY HOLIDAY

Work Schedule

SCHEDULE SUMMARY

PROJECT Melville-144 AREA SP RELEASE 1 DATE 9/15/X6 PAGE 1

ACTIVITY DESCRIPTION	ACTIVITY NUMBER	PLANNED DURATION	EARLY		LATE		FLOAT
			START	FINISH	START	FINISH	
SP-Trenches & Grade Beams	17	10	9-16-X6	9-28-X6	10-16-X6	10-28-X6	00

WORK ORDER	COST CODE	DESCRIPTION	UNIT OF MEASURE	VOLUME	ESTIMATED LABOR				ASSIGNMENTS					
					UNITS / HOUR	RATE / HOUR	TOTAL HOURS	TOTAL COST	DATE	VOLUME	DATE	VOLUME	DATE	VOLUME
00107	000001	Relocate S&PExit												
ACTIVITY TOTAL ▶														

FIGURE 36

accomplished in the absence of one. The identification of exceptions, so vital to cost control, will not be as valid or dramatic, but will afford management an opportunity to make decisions prior to the impossible being undertaken or, more important, being paid for. In this respect, some contractors attempt to complete a project in the same manner as placing nine one-month pregnant women in a hospital and expecting them collectively to produce a baby in one month.

Another method of accomplishing this same objective is to use a computer to list all the components of the detailed estimate to prepare a work schedule. A simple project, such as a home, requires only an undetailed list, such as is seen in Figure 36. The more complex the project, the more detailed the support information must be.

Again, in some projects only the phases would be necessary to establish a Management by Exception System. A sewer and water contractor in a small town is an example. A more complex project would require the addition of steps as subdivisions of the phases. This has been illustrated in the example of the home builder. In our last example of a complex industrial construction project, phases and steps are not sufficient, so the actual estimated components are added. A good rule of thumb to use in determining the detail of the initial plan is the amount of time, in both labor and calendar, and dollars to be expended. The contractor laying a water pipe system may have trenched the entire line in two days. This trenching may represent 20% of the total dollars and labor of the project. Here, trenching would be a phase, controllable for purposes of exception management as a single unit. Both the time and dollar amounts are small. The same contractor may, on the other hand, contract to construct a major water line half way across the state. If such is the case, the phase of trenching would span forty weeks. The necessity to plan the steps and perhaps the components should become quickly apparent. Yet, the trenching would still contribute 20% to the total project.

Once the Work Schedule has been accomplished, the project manager is in a position of assigning work to each of his general and skill foremen. By exception the project has been reduced to a workable plan.

Weekly and/or daily assignments are then part of a whole, rather than parallel or unrelated components. This aspect of Management by Exception at the execution point is now and only now possible. The progress of the weekly and daily progress has had the major exceptions removed. Materials can now be available on time. Equipment can be brought into play when needed without waiting.

EXECUTING THE PLAN

Construction foremen dislike paper work almost as much as anyone else. Thus, only the goals and completion objectives should be spelled out in the

Weekly Schedule. Figure 37 reflects a typical weekly schedule given to a foreman for work assignment and exception reporting of the obstacles he encounters.

As the project flows from the Detailed Estimate down to the Daily Allocation of Manpower, Material & Equipment, the project is at the basic level of exception reporting. The build-up of the Daily Foremen Exceptions can be detailed and built up to alert management to hidden problems in all aspects of the overall commitment.

Here, once again, the predetermined categories of exceptions must be established by management before execution, or the reports would become about as confusing as the construction reports from the original tower of Babel. In Figure 37, the individual foreman extracts his assignment from the Schedule Summary or Work Schedule. Only the basic information is listed. The foreman reports daily by phase, step or component his consumption of manpower and work accomplished. Exceptions are noted through a stroke tally by predetermined categories daily by the foreman. The subjective exceptions as differentiated from the real exceptions quickly pop out when the individual formen report, as against the group they are teamed with, or one project being compared with the other (as shown in Figure 38).

In the example of the small home builder, the same steps apply, only a simpler method. Figure 35 shows a simple Ghant graph method of taking the detailed estimate and reworking it to an on-site schedule. One can add the exceptions to be detailed at the bottom of the schedule in the same identical manner. The management of these homes being built is afforded a close scrutiny of his skills and foremen, in the same manner as the management of the industrial contractor can look at his.

The large and small contractors covered in this chapter have established true control over their construction projects through the use of this Management by Exception System. The homebuilder realized his anticipated profits. The large industrial contractor doubled his business and profit. Neither did so without understanding and applying all the rules of the preceding chapters. The financial aspects of Management by Exception have been omitted here to be covered in the chapter on Management by Exception in the Financial Aspect of the Business.

MANAGEMENT BY EXCEPTION POINTERS

A. Review of construction methods
   1. A bid or estimate initials any project.
   2. Bids are made in the absence of blueprints.
   3. Bids are formulated from past projects.
   4. If no cost frame system of Management by Exception exists, profits may not exist either.

Foreman's Work Schedule

PROJECT Melville - 144

WORK CLASSIFICATION Concrete

PREPARED BY S. Melton - Supt.

WEEKLY PLAN & OPERATING REPORT

FOREMAN J. Jones

PLANNED THIS WEEK							ACTUALLY ACCOMPLISHED (MANHOURS USED / VOLUME COMPLETED)						
WORK ORDER NUMBER	AREA	COST CODE	WORK DESCRIPTION	PLANNED EARNED HOURS	PLANNED UNIT VOLUME	UNIT OF MEASURE	MON.	TUES.	WED.	THURS.	FRI.	SAT.	SUN
0004	A-1	003310	Hand Level Floor Area Column Line A-1 To H-1	100	400	SFT	210' / 45	190' / 50					
0005	A-1	003310	Pour Slab On Grade A-1 To H-1	40	400	SFT			400' / 36				
0006	A-1	003310	Broom Finish Slab A-1 To H-1	20	400	SFT			400' / 23				
0009	A-1	003320	Form Box Outs A-3 To H-3	10	10	EA				10 / 11			
0013	A-1	003330	Pour Column # 13,14,15	30	3	EA				2 / 36			

EXCEPTIONS:

	M	T	W	T	F	S	S
A. LACK OF MATERIALS		I				I	
B. DRAWING CHANGES			I				
C. PRIORITY CHANGES							
D. LACK OF DRAWINGS		I	I	I			
E. EQUIPMENT BREAKDOWN							
F. LACK OF EQUIPMENT OR PROPER TOOLS							
G. REWORK				I			
H. TEMPERATURE TOO LOW							
I. INSUFFICIENT MANPOWER, SKILLS							
J. WAIT FOR SUBS							
K. POOR SITE CONDITIONS (MUD, ETC.)							

FIGURE 37

Comparative Foremen Exceptions

EXCEPTIONS	FOREMEN																TOTAL
	JKS	DPS	PJK	WDC	BAM	BMA	LAP	FDR	LA	CTT							
A. LACK OF MATERIALS	4	1	—	—	3	5	—	1	1	5							20
B. & D. CHANGES & LACK OF DRAWINGS	1	—	—	4	1	1	2	1	3	2							15
C. PRIORITY CHANGES	—	—	—	1	—	—	—	—	—	—							1
E. EQUIPMENT BREAKDOWN	6	5	4	—	—	3	4	2	10	6							40
F. LACK OF EQUIPMENT OR PROPER TOOLS	11	9	6	9	2	9	4	3	2	5							60
G. REWORK	—	—	1	—	—	1	—	—	1	—							3
H. TEMPERATURE TOO LOW	—	—	—	—	—	—	—	—	—	—							0
I. INSUFFICIENT MANPOWER. SKILLS	1	—	—	—	—	1	—	—	—	—							2
J. WAIT FOR SUBS	5	1	—	1	—	—	—	1	—	—							8
K. POOR SITE CONDITIONS (MUD. ETC.)	—	—	—	2	—	1	—	—	3	—							6
L. RAIN DAYS	—	—	—	2	—	—	1	—	—	—							3

FIGURE 38

B. First Step in establishing a Management by Exception system is to phase estimate, which is used as a check point for time and dollar costs.

C. A plan must be in place before any attempt can be made to manage by exception.

D. Detail estimates

E. Establish a work schedule by re-stacking the detailed estimate.

F. Execute Work Schedule.

9

MANAGEMENT BY EXCEPTION IN THE FINANCIAL OPERATION OF THE BUSINESS

MANAGEMENT BY EXCEPTION IN ACCOUNTING

When it comes to the financial aspect of a business, the systems man must, by necessity, tread cautiously, as he is entering the sacred realm of the accountant. While the author acknowledges their field of expertise and value of worth to the company, they are in as dire need of good system as any of the other disciplines in the firm.

Managing Inventory, Manpower, Material and Machines by Exception will produce dramatic results. But alas, these may never be reflected in the P & L unless similar techniques are applied to the final pay point, as reflected in the accounting aspect of the company.

In the area of accounting, such as accounts payable, accounts receivable, payroll, production and inventory costing, almost no attempt is made to establish a plan prior to execution. Yet, the need for a Management by Exception System should be evident.

SYNCHRONIZE ACCOUNTING TO THE REST OF THE COMPANY

Earlier in the book an illustration was given where the work load and the time for performing the work were not synchronized. In accounting, as related to the other operations of a firm, this same type of offset schedule may very often be the case. Promotion, Production and Accounting may all be set on different cycles or cutoffs. An example may be seen when a store operation develops and releases the week's ad campaign prior to Wednesday of each week. This is noted by the extra large newspaper edition we all look at on Wednesday evening or Thursday morning. The ads for the grocery industry hit for the weekend traffic. The following ads of Fridays, Mondays and Tuesdays are written with the big mid-week push in mind. Here, all the work load is built around the Wednesday/Thursday ads. So logically, the promotion departments work week slacks off Thursday morning. Their week runs from Wednesday through the following Tuesday.

The production of the retail stores themselves follow the ads and reflect the ads and reflect a far greater demand at the end of the week, than at the first. Yet, payrolls are cycled from midnight Sunday morning until Saturday night. With this in mind, when should the accounting cycle for the week cut off? If you thought the cutoff should be Saturday night at midnight or Wednesday at midnight, you would be wrong in most cases. Sunday afternoon at 3:00 P.M. in one of the largest chains in the West Coast is the accounting cut-off date. Here, then, is the problem of setting up a Management by Exception System for the managers of the firm. Any report will not be able to relate Promotion, Production and Accounting without breaking or interrupting the other's cycle. Obviously, a change has to be made, or no accurate Management by Exception System will evolve. The accountability of the facts will be missing. The real flow of business should be determined prior to establishing the cycles and cutoffs. In the case cited, a compromise was made and Saturday at midnight was the universal cutoff throughout the company. Now, when the management reads the comparative figures for promotion, labor and sales, they all reflect the same time span. In the past each represented a part of the other. Once this had been done, a comparison of weeks became easier. Further, the inter-relation of sales, service and accounting could be used to reflect problems by exception.

Once the various entities of an operation are on the same cycle, a relationship evolves which helps pinpoint exceptions or areas that require management attention.

INTER-RELATIONS MARK EXCEPTIONS

In one of our nation's largest industrial laundries, this re-establishing of all the cutoff cycles allowed management to look at the cost relationships between sales, service (the route trucks), production (the processing plant) and their cash flow (the accounting functions).

Once the cycles were set on the same cutoff, it was very quickly ascertained by management the relationship between the operating areas. See Figure 39. One dollar of sales would generate 16¢ of labor in production. Accounting should show cash deposits for the same time period of one dollar. Figure 40 is a simple circle showing the basic operations of the firm. Using the example of the industrial laundry and applying the relationships between the operations, one can identify the exceptions as soon as the plan is made. Assuming the plan to be in correct relationship, an exception will be quickly identified when the actual is plotted. Figure 40 is an example. Here the plan was consistent with the ratio pattern, but the actual reflected a large exception in the manufacturing area.

Once the inter-relationships between operations of a firm have been established, false reporting can be identified through this knowledge. As each department or operation prepares its own reports and only top management sees the total of all the operations, the exceptions jump out quickly.

Interdiscipline Ratios

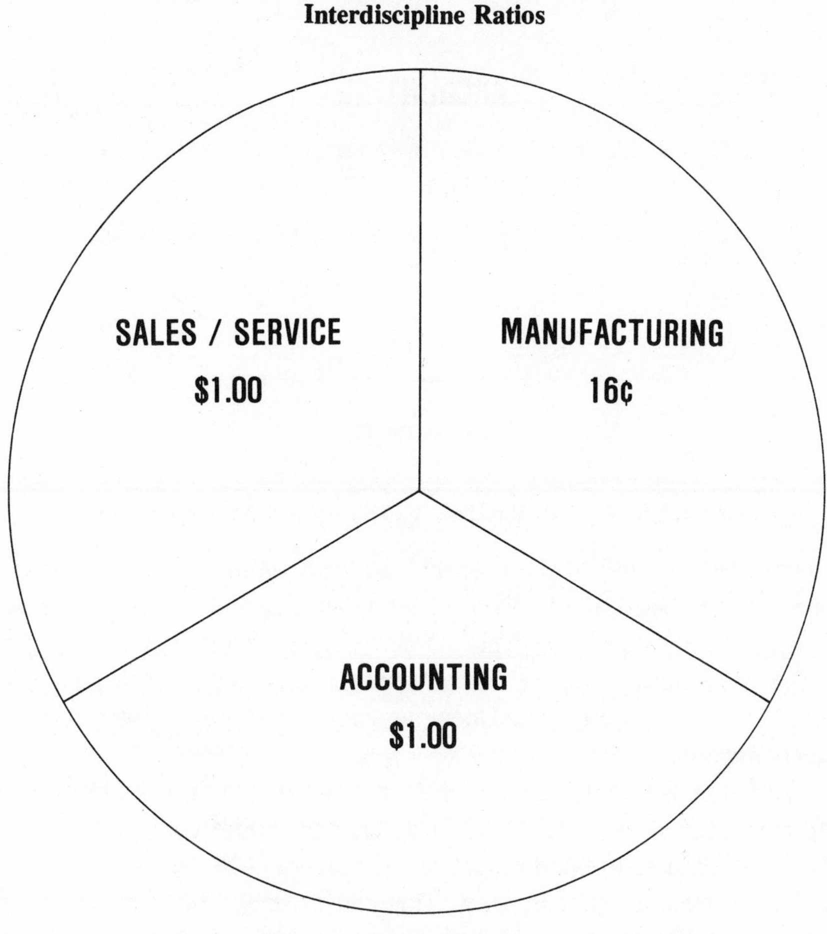

FIGURE 39

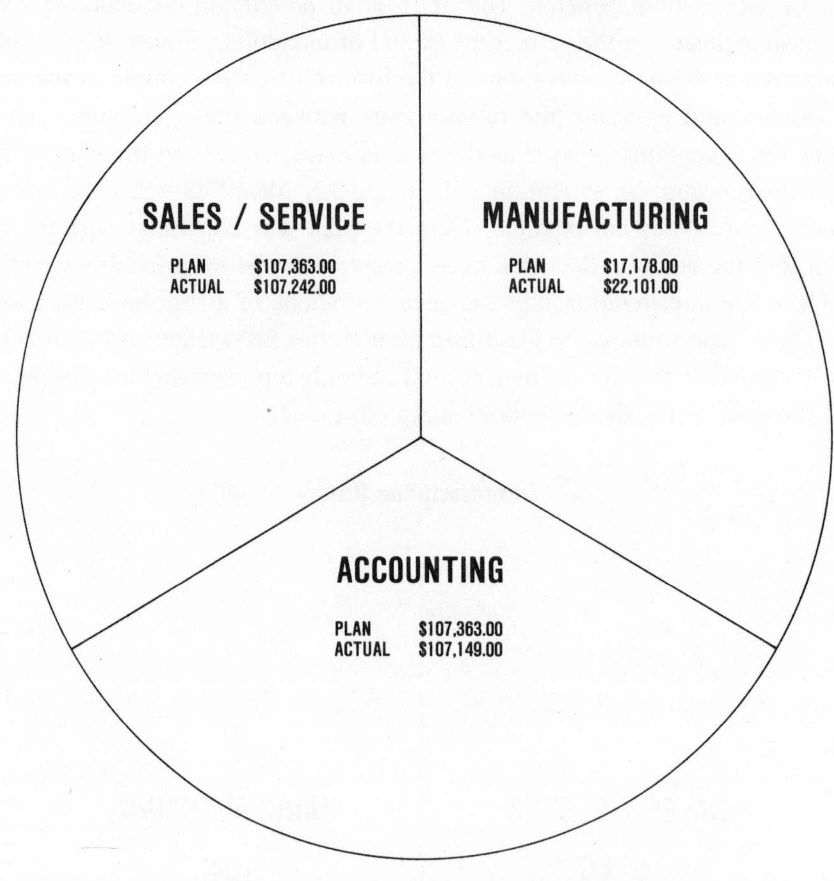

FIGURE 40

ACCOUNTING PERIODS, MONTHS AND QUARTERS

So far, we have talked about getting the week on the same cycle. Once this has been accomplished, the problem of the month, period or quarter comes into play. Most weekly reports feed into larger reports for the month, and quarter. Here the government imposes requirements such as the Quarterly Wage Report—941, the Quarterly State Unemployment Tax Report or many more of the increasing reports.

An accounting calendar should be set up. But first, a decision must be made by top management as to what will best serve the entire company, as far as a cutoff time. Almost always the accounting function will set the time independently of the flow of the company. This causes undue pressure on the other operations and allows the accounting function to exercise a larger control over the operation than is necessary. This method of fitting the company to the accountants' schedule is placing the cart before the corporate horse.

Take the example where the month is accounted on a true calander month with the cutoff being Thursday this month. Sales and manufacturing reports will not fit, for comparative purposes, when last year's figures are compared with this year's.

Some firms will seek to rectify this problem by making the cutoffs on the last Friday of the month. This helps but isn't sufficient due, once again, to the need to compare one month to another. A simple method is to establish 13 periods of four weeks each. This method may be argued against by the accountants, but the decision should be made by top management in charge of all the company's operation.

Once the weeks and periods are set, the relationships between operations, periods and years become much easier. Heretofore undetected exceptions will emerge. Questions will be asked, and the road to management involvement in improvement will be forthcoming.

EXCEPTIONS IN PAYROLL, ACCOUNTS RECEIVABLES AND ACCOUNTS PAYABLES

Once the weeks and periods have been established, a drive to level the cash demands with the revenue can be brought into focus. If the accounting periods are the same, management can ask, why does the payroll vary? Figure 41 reflects a typical recap of hours in an operation. The months are all irregular. In this

Hours Report

Month	*First Year*	*Second Year*
January	54,157	44,437
February	43,318	42,284
March	46,742	52,556
April	55,176	42,523
May	45,995	42,822
June	47,811	54,807
July	61,554	42,905
August	44,483	43,301
September	43,799	52,212
October	53,167	42,909
November	42,138	42,026
December	51,764	50,147
Total	590,104	552,929

FIGURE 41

example the company's accounting was set to cut the month on full weeks. In one year January would have four weeks, the next year five. No periods were set, and comparison becomes difficult. Figure 42 reflects these same figures set on 13 periods for the year. Note the ease with which a manager can highlight the exception period, now that he knows it reports the same time span. These figures show the hours paid in the company. The same lack of clear comparison is true if you were reporting payroll, receivables, payables, production or any other set of figures used by management to highlight exceptions.

Hours Report

Period	*First Year*	*Second Year*
1	43,326	44,437
2	43,319	42,284
3	45,885	42,044
4	44,789	42,404
5	45,068	42,749
6	46,904	43,589
7	48,526	43,374
8	59,172	43,100
9	44,145	42,498
10	43,166	42,096
11	42,434	42,688
12	41,958	41,500
13	41,412	40,116
Total	590,104	552,929

FIGURE 42

For further Management by Exception application, the planned figures should be included. Figure 43 uses the same figures as Figure 42 and adds the Plan for the hours to be used.

Now the manager has the ability to see the comparisons from period to period, year against year. In addition the question is answered as to how well is he doing as compared to the Plan. If the manager had a total Management by Exception System in effect, he could dig out the specific problems and apply solutions.

As in almost all statistical recaps, such as we have shown, the pure figures themselves only direct attention to the exceptions. If the pay point (sales, units produced, tonnage shipped) figures are added to the original figures, variances may be explained on the face of the report. Figure 44 reflects the addition of volume and the relationship between payroll hours to further highlight exceptions. The plan figures for payroll, volume and ratio have been eliminated for this example. Here, it will be noted the high payroll hours were in some cases offset by high sales figures, therefore explaining in advance the question which might have arisen when one looked at Figure 42 or 43. Also note how good the figures look when compared to last year, looking at the figures without the volume. Yet, with the addition of volume, some of the lower figures are not low enough. And, many of the high figures are well justified because of the volume produced.

Hours Report

Period	*Plan*	*First Year Actual*	*Plan*	*Second Year Actual*
1	42,000	43,326	42,000	44,437
2	42,000	43,319	42,000	42,284
3	42,000	45,885	42,000	42,044
4	42,000	44,789	42,000	42,404
5	42,000	45,068	42,000	42,749
6	42,000	46,904	42,000	43,589
7	42,000	48,526	42,000	43,374
8	42,000	59,172	42,000	43,100
9	42,000	44,145	42,000	42,489
10	42,000	43,166	42,000	42,096
11	42,000	42,434	42,000	42,688
12	42,000	41,958	42,000	41,550
13	42,000	41,412	42,000	40,116
Total	546,000	590,104	546,000	552,929

FIGURE 43

Hours Report

Period	*First Year*		*$ Per*	*Second Year*		*$ Per*
	Hours	*Volume*	*Hour*	*Hours*	*Volume*	*Hour*
1	43,326	1,902,342	43.91	44,437	1,895,417	42.65
2	43,319	1,972,696	45.54	42,284	1,889,644	44.69
3	45,885	2,000,037	43.59	42,044	1,970,680	46.87
4	44,789	1,908,127	42.60	42,404	1,913,479	45.12
5	45,068	1,925,567	42.73	42,749	1,912,925	44.75
6	46,904	1,942,488	41.41	43,589	1,847,075	42.37
7	48,526	2,177,715	44.88	43,374	1,896,168	43.72
8	59,172	1,999,291	33.79	43,100	2,002,678	46.46
9	44,145	1,867,700	42.31	42,498	1,913,970	45.04
10	43,166	1,876,485	43.47	42,096	1,974,898	46.91
11	42,434	1,833,719	43.21	42,688	1,862,446	43.63
12	41,958	1,775,563	42.32	41,550	1,986,691	47.81
13	41,412	1,957,768	47.28	40,116	1,941,345	48.39
Total	590,104	25,139,498	42.60	552,929	25,007,416	45.23

FIGURE 44

If one wanted to have weekly or daily reports fed into Figure 44, it would be necessary to do so on the same accounting periods. Figure 45 is an example of all the operations of a firm reporting the total picture each week, including the reason for the variances. Here, the base figures are last year's figures for the same period. The production is reporting in standard hours of production due to the various types of production in the 16 plants reporting. This example reflects the top management report of an entire company covering five states. Each week the president knows the complete status of his firm, cash flow, payroll, sales and the reasons why the exceptions occurred.

WHEN ACCOUNTING DOLLARS DON'T TELL THE WHOLE STORY

With the cost of labor, goods and services on the rise, many times the comparison of pure dollars will lead management to believe they have no exceptions when, in truth, they have exceptions which should be corrected at once.

Like the method of "square foot" estimated build-up through long division of the last project, so are production norms built for management by the accountants. These methods of long division conclusions doom management to improvements of a minor nature. The oft stated positive or negative production variance so readily on the tip of management's tongue really only speaks of how good it is compared to last year's averages which may or may not have been correct to start with.

Once again the basics still apply—even though dealing this time in money. What are the planned costs of the production? Not, how well are we doing against last year's average?

CASE IN POINT

A small Midwest manufacturer of a food product compared his cost of production from year to year on the average norm of his past years. His raw material and labor continued to rise. His profit decreased, yet his comparison was better and better than his past year's. A simple stack up of standard cost data reflected his improvement had fallen far short of his cost increases. From the outset he had failed to establish a solid financial cost plan as it applied to his current labor and material costs. Once established, his attention was fully directed towards the accomplishment of a positive picture, one he knew he must achieve. Thus, he was not lulled into believing he was good enough to cover costs, merely because he was doing better than last year.

Figure 46 reflects a grocery cost index established to translate the dollar per man hour figure used by many grocers in evaluating individual store and chain performance. The use of this or similar indices takes the fickle dollar per, used by

Integrated Plan, Hours, Volume Ratio, Exceptions, Management Report

DISTRIBUTE TO: PRESIDENT
NORTHERN DIVISION MANAGER
SOUTHERN DIVISION MANAGER

MANAGEMENT REPORT

WEEK ENDING ____________

	AREAS	MANAGEMENT	NUMBER OF EMPLOYEES		EMPLOYEES HOURS			VOLUME				PERFORMANCE RATIO	PERFORMANCE		
			PLAN	ACTUAL	BASE	PLAN	ACTUAL	UNIT OF MEASURE	BASE	PLAN	ACTUALLY COMPLETED		BASE	PLAN	ACTUAL
SALES & SERVICE	OHIO				2520			SALES DOLLARS	86777			SALES PER MANHOURS	34.4		
	KENTUCKY				1677			SALES DOLLARS	49647				29.6		
	GEORGIA				1600			SALES DOLLARS	50335				31.5		
	FLORIDA				1864			SALES DOLLARS	41491				22.3		
	S. CAROLINA				1283			SALES DOLLARS	26903				26.8		
	TOTAL ALL SALES				8924			SALES DOLLARS	255153				29.5		
PLANTS	OHIO				5973			STANDARD HOURS	2640			MANHOURS PER STANDARD HOUR	2.3		
	KENTUCKY				2991			STANDARD HOURS	1960				1.5		
	GEORGIA				4515			STANDARD HOURS	1528				2.9		
	FLORIDA				2774			STANDARD HOURS	967				2.9		
	S. CAROLINA				1257			STANDARD HOURS	488				2.6		
	TOTAL ALL PLANTS				17510			STANDARD HOURS	7583				2.3		
OFFICE ADMINISTRATION	OHIO				1094			CASH DEPOSITS	86777			DOLLARS DEPOSITED PER MANHOUR	79.32		
	KENTUCKY				353			CASH DEPOSITS	49647				140.64		
	GEORGIA				410			CASH DEPOSITS	50335				122.76		
	FLORIDA				339			CASH DEPOSITS	41491				122.39		
	S. CAROLINA				200			CASH DEPOSITS	26903				134.52		
	CORPORATE				—			NOT APPLICABLE	—				—		
	DATA PROCESSING				405			NOT APPLICABLE	—				—		
	TOTAL OFFICE & ADMIN.				2801			CASH DEPOSITS	255153				91.09		
	TOTAL COMPANY				29235			SALES DOLLARS	255153			SALES PER MANHOUR	8.73		

— EXCEPTIONS —

PLANTS	OH	NC	GA	FL	SC
MACHINE BREAKDOWN	—	—	—	—	—
LACK OF MATERIALS	—	—	—	—	—
REWASH	—	—	—	—	—
OTHER	—	—	—	—	—

SALES / SERVICE	OH	NC	GA	FL	SC
INCORRECT INVOICES	—	—	—	—	—
EQUIPMENT BREAKDOWN	—	—	—	—	—
SHORTAGES	—	—	—	—	—
ACCOUNT QUITS — NUMBER	—	—	—	—	—
ACCOUNT QUITS — DOLLARS	—	—	—	—	—
NEW ACCOUNTS — NUMBER	—	—	—	—	—
NEW ACCOUNTS — DOLLARS	—	—	—	—	—
ROUTE DELIVERY PROBLEMS	—	—	—	—	—
OTHER	—	—	—	—	—

OFFICE	OH	NC	GA	FL	SC
POOR INFORMATION FROM SALES	—	—	—	—	—
WAIT FOR DATA PROCESSING	—	—	—	—	—
CAN'T MATCH PAYMENT/INVOICE	—	—	—	—	—
WAIT INFO OUTLYING AREAS	—	—	—	—	—
CUSTOMER COMPLAINTS	—	—	—	—	—
OTHER	—	—	—	—	—

FIGURE 45

so many managers, and brings it back to a constant value. Therefore, while $38 per man hour was great when eggs were 49¢ a dozen and labor $2.85 per hour, how good is $49 per man hour two years later, when eggs are now 89¢ a dozen and labor is $4.75 per hour?

Grocery Index

Grocery Item			**Base Cost**	**Cost**
Description	*No*	*Size*		
ALUMINUM FOIL—REYNOLDS	24	75′		
AMMONIA—Housebrand	18	QT.		
APRICOTS—DELMONTE	24	17 OZ.		
BABY CEREAL—GERBERS	12	8 OZ.		
BABY FOOD—GERBERS	24	3-1/2 OZ.		
BAKED BEANS—B&M	24	19 OZ.		
BAKING SODA—CLABBER GIRL	24	10 OZ.		
BLEACH—CLOROX	6	1 GAL.		
CAT FOOD—FRISKIES	24	6-1/2 OZ.		
CATSUP—HUNTS	24	14 OZ.		
CEREAL—KELLOGGS	24	18 OZ.		
CHILI CON CARNE—GEBHARDT	24	300		
COFFEE—MJB	24	1 LB.		
CORN—DEL MONTE	24	303		
CORN BEEF HASH—ARMOUR	24	15-1/2 OZ.		
CRACKERS—THIN FLAKE	6	1 LB.		
DOG FOOD—FRISKIES	5	10 LB.		
DRESSING—WISHBONE (FRENCH)	12	8 OZ.		
FLOUR—GOLD METAL	15	5 LB.		
GREEN BEANS—GREEN GIANT	24	303		
JELLO (LIME)	48	3 OZ.		
KOOL-AID (RASPBERRY)	72	PKG.		
MACARONI—Housebrand	12	1 LB.		
MAYONNAISE—BEST FOODS	24	16 OZ.		
NAPKINS—SCOTKINS	48	PKG.		
OLEOMARGARINE—BLUE BONNET	30	1 LB.		
PEACH HALVES—LIBBY	24	303		
PEANUT BUTTER—SKIPPY	12	28 OZ.		
PEAS—GREEN GIANT	24	303		
PEAS—LIBBY	24	VAC.		
PEAS—JACK & BEAN STALK	24	303		
PICKLES—DEL MONTE	12	22 OZ.		
PORK & BEANS—CAMPBELLS	24	28 OZ.		
RICE—MINUTE	24	14 OZ.		

FIGURE 46

Grocery Item			Base Cost	Cost
SANITARY NAPKINS—KOTEX	12	24 PKG.		
SHORTENING—CRISCO	12	3 LB.		
SOAPS—AJAX	6	BOXES		
SOUP—CAMPBELLS (TOMATO)	48	8 OZ.		
SUGAR—C&H	12	5 LB.		
TOILET PAPER—AURORA	24	PKG.		
Sub Total–Staples	DOLLARS			
	Percent			
DEVILED HAMS—UNDERWOOD	48	2 OZ.		
DIXIE CUPS	12	9 OZ.		
PANTY HOSE	3	PKG.		
PICKLED PIGS FEET—HORMEL	12	9 OZ.		
POTATOES—SHOESTRING, FRENCH	12	7 OZ.		
RAVIOLIS—CHEF BOY-AR-DEE	24	15-1/2 OZ.		
SARAN WRAP	24	50"		
SMOKED OYSTERS—DUNBAR	24	8 OZ.		
Sub Total–Impulse	DOLLARS			
	PERCENT			
Total Staples & Impulse	DOLLARS			
	PERCENT			

FIGURE 46 (continued)

CONTROLLING LABOR COSTS IN A MANAGEMENT BY EXCEPTION SYSTEM

While many industries have the possibility only of minor control over the cost of their materials or machines, almost all have the ability to control the labor they add to produce their product. Yet, almost never does one find a system whereby management works out a plan as to what dollars are to be paid in any given week.

The accounting reports that abound in companies almost always lack the single insertion of the plan column on the payroll recap, accounts payable records, aged accounts receivable reports and all the rest of the many accounting reports. Since this omission exists, why call them reports? They are only recaps. In the absence of a plan, how could management reflect an exception of a single incident except through other knowledge, memory or intuition?

IDENTIFYING THE FRINGE BENEFIT AS A LABOR COST

One of the least known costs in labor is the cost of the hidden or fringe benefit. Management may talk of signing a contract with the union whereby the new labor cost will be $5.25 per hour. This cost may well represent less than two-thirds of the total cost of those labor hours. The payroll register and the many management information systems evolving from them will reflect only the pay given to the employee directly. That same contract just signed with the union may have more fringe benefit percentage-wise than the labor rate itself. The systems man can watch the results of his Management by Exception efforts dissipate if he isn't alert to the cost of all the fringe benefits each labor hour would represent. Accounting, in most cases, is so complex that no single individual has ever worked out the total cost of the fringe value in many companies. The reason, again, is that no plan was ever in place, no comparison to the actual, therefore, no exceptions. In the case of fringe, the systems man may well have to go to several different sources to determine the full cost of the package. As an example, the 20 pound turkey given to all plant employees at Christmas seems innocent enough, until you realize it adds .006 per hour to each hour worked in the plant for the whole year. In the last ten years social security employer added amount has gone from 4.2% with a base salary of $6,600 to 5.85% with a base salary of $15,300. This means the employer used to pay $277.20 in an average year for social security. Now this same employer would have to pay $895.05. When one looks at the cost per hour as a fringe benefit (granted it is a federally imposed benefit, but a benefit all the same), the cost has gone from 14¢ per hour to 45¢. This example applies to a worker earning $3.30 in 1966 to the same worker earning $7.65 in 1976. These figures reveal the subtlety of fringe in an inflationary economy. The above salary increase is 236%, but the fringe benefit increased by 329%. Because of the loss of identity of the fringe benefit, the systems man may well have to repeat his readings every quarter or six months. And, at worst, just prior to negotiating the new contract for labor. Figure 47 is a check sheet to dig out the hidden costs of these fringe packages. Once this job has been accomplished, compare this cost to the stated labor rate. Once the true cost of each hour of labor has been established, the generally accepted figures used in planning the company may have to be altered. Fringe benefit identification may come as the largest exception ever handled by the company management.

CASE IN POINT

A large retail firm with 74 outlets offered the public 24 hour shopping in over half of its outlets. This firm, like most, computed its labor cost on raw hourly rate. The logic looked good, but the profit wasn't there. When a study of the fringe benefit cost per labor hour was developed by a systems team, the president shut down all 24 hour operations. The reason for the missing profit had been discovered. In this example, labor had been figured at $3.30 per hour. It was assumed a

SOURCE:	COMPANY:
Cost of Fringe Benefits	
DATE:	LOCATION:

Benefit Description	*Date*
FEDERAL & STATE STATUTORY REQUIREMENT BENEFITS	
Federal & State Unemployment Tax	
Federal Social Security Tax (Employer's Portion Only)	
Overtime Premium (Premium Portion Only)	
Workmen's Compensation Premium	
Sub Total	
FRINGE BENEFITS	
Christmas or Year-End Bonus	
Paid Vacations	
Pensions & Retirement	
Paid Unworked Holidays	
Pay for Unworked Time (voting time, jury duty, blood bank, excused absences, military, birthdays, etc.)	
Group Health & Accident Insurance	
Group Life Insurance	
Group Hospitalization Insurance	
Sick Benefits	
Paid Lunch Periods	
Rest Periods (Scheduled Only)	
Wash-Up Time (Scheduled Only)	
Severance and Separation Pay	
Shift Premium Pay	
Supplemental Unemployment Benefits	
Make-Up Pay	
Sub Total	
COMPANY CONVENIENCES & EMPLOYEE INDIRECT BENEFITS	
Subsidies for Cafeteria or Commissary Operation or other promotions benefiting employees—vending machines	
Dispensary Service	
Physical Examinations	
Educational Programs	

FIGURE 47

Benefit Description	*Date*
Training Program (Other than on the job)	
Transfer Expense	
Uniforms, Safety Clothing, Personal Protective Devices	
Employee's Paper or Magazine Expense	
Employee's Parking Lot Expense	
Length of Service Awards & Suggestion Awards	
Lost Time and Group Fall-Down	
Paid Time—Contract Negotiations	
Paid Time—Grievance Procedure	
Recreational & Athletic Activities, Picnics, Parties	
Lost Income from Cafeteria Space	
Sub Total	
Grand Total	

FIGURE 47 (continued)

profit would be maintained if labor kept under 11% of sales. This ratio was true upon its application to the total operating costs of the chain itself. When the Hours & Dollars volume of the night time operation were isolated, the percentage dropped to 5%, due to the overhead spread. When the fringe package, which included a premium pay for the night time hours, was added up, the total cost of the extended store hours ran as high as 20% of the sales dollars. The base pay rate carried a 15% graveyard shift premium and so did so many of the other fringes tied into the labor rate, such as social security.

Once again, the total dollars may not be sufficient to pop out the exceptions. The systems man should scrutinize all aspects of accounting to determine if a valid plan is being laid side by side to the actual reports, and collect the exceptions to carry them forward to management for action. The methods to be used are the same as those in controlling all other elements of a company.

FINANCIAL STATEMENTS WITH A PLAN, ACTUAL AND EXCEPTIONS

What a boon it would be to the average investor if the accountants preparing financial statements were required to use a Management by Exception system. Look at almost any set of financial statements, and you will note the simple method of identifying exceptions, as shown in Figure 45, is missing.

In looking at as many annual reports as you wish, you will never find a plan listed next to the balance sheet or profit and loss statements. Figure 48 takes a

Typical Balance Sheet

December 31, 19

ASSETS	
Current Assets	
Cash and certificates of deposit	$ 2,800,999
Marketable securities—at cost which approximates market	371,896
Accounts receivable—less allowances of $139,436 in 19	790,381
Supplies and other	649,100
Total current assets	4,612,376
Property, Plant and Equipment—At cost less accumulated depreciation	12,909,436
Intangible Assets—At cost less amortization	12,464,804
Deferred System Costs	128,280
Other Assets	562,527
Total	$30,677,423
LIABILITIES	
Current Liabilities	
Notes payable due within one year	
Accounts payable and accrued liabilities	$ 1,077,787
Federal income tax	163,597
Deferred income	519,852
Total current liabilities	1,761,236
Notes Payable	17,695,000
Deferred Federal Income Tax	363,525
Minority Interests in Subsidiaries	116,265
Stockholder's Equity	
Common Stock—authorized, 5,000,000 shares of $1 par value; outstanding, 3,555,125 in 19	3,555,125
Additional paid-in capital	5,582,564
Retained earnings	1,603,708
Total stockholders' equity	10,741,397
Total	$30,677,423

See accompanying summary of significant accounting policies and notes.

FIGURE 48

Typical Balance Sheet with Plan

December 31, 19	Plan	Actual
ASSETS		
Current Assets		
Cash and certificates of deposit	$ 3,500,000	$ 2,800,999
Marketable securities—at cost which approximates market	400,000	371,896
Accounts receivable—less allowances of $139,436 in 19	800,000	790,381
Supplies and other	500,000	649,100
Total current assets	5,200,000	4,612,376
Property, Plant, and Equipment—At cost less accumulated depreciation	12,909,436	12,909,436
Intangible Assets—At cost less amortization	12,464,804	12,464,804
Deferred System Costs	100,000	128,280
Other Assets	503,183	562,527
Total	$31,177,423	$30,677,423
LIABILITIES		
Current Liabilities		
Notes payable due within one year		
Accounts payable and accrued liabilities	$ 1,000,000	$ 1,077,787
Federal income tax	100,000	163,597
Deferred income	519,852	519,852
Total current liabilities	1,619,852	1,761,236
Notes Payable	17,000,000	17,695,000
Deferred Federal Income Tax	363,525	363,525
Minority Interests in Subsidiaries	100,000	116,265
Stockholders' Equity		
Common stock—authorized, 5,000,000 shares of $1 par value outstanding 3,555,125 in 19	3,555,125	3,555,125
Additional paid in capital	5,000,000	5,582,564
Retained earnings	3,538,921	1,603,708
Total stockholders' equity	12,094,046	10,741,397
Total	$31,177,423	$30,677,423

See accompanying summary of significant exceptions and what caused them.

FIGURE 49

balance sheet from a typical annual report. Note the usual note at the bottom of the report, "See accompanying summary of significant accounting policies and notes." Here is the pinnacle of reporting in the business world—the worth of the company!

Figure 49 reflects what financial reports would look like in a Management by Exception system. Note, for purposes of this example, how the balance sheet looks when last year's budget was placed in front of the figures. This same approach could be applied to the statement of changes in financial position, financial summaries and all the other sheets in a corporation financial package. While this approach may not appear practical to show to the shareholders, at least top management should use it for their own monthly and quarterly reports. So down through the entire operation of the company there is a Management by Exception system. It has been established to identify problems and force solutions. As the beginning of this book we talked of a definition of Management by Exception. "Management by Exception is a method of using exceptions to control the operation. It can be the culmination of an operating system, where interruptions to the completion of a plan are identified at the point of initial execution. These interruptions of exceptions can be collected and carried forward to all levels of management. If properly identified and grouped, these exceptions can be either eliminated or must be included in future plans. Management by Exception is the method of making management face the impact of problems."

If the system is built upon sound planning, and each department, operation and discipline are included in the system, then top management in that company would have no fear of listing its overall plan against its financial reports for its shareholders. If such is not the case, the forms and techniques covered in this handbook should be placed in use at once.

MANAGEMENT BY EXCEPTION POINTERS

1. Accounting, like any other area, can be controlled by a Management by Exception System.
2. Synchronize accounting to the rest of the company:
   a. Identify the cycles and cutoffs.
   b. Establish the same cutoff for every department.
3. Management can then compare sales, service and accounting on a realistic basis.
4. Problems will be reflected by exception through these comparisons.
5. Use equal periods, not months, for a realistic comparison—profits, hours, volume, etc., from period to period, year to year.
6. Accounting dollars can be deceptive; therefore, costs must be planned for.

7. Labor costs can be controlled through proper planning.
8. Fringe benefits should be included in labor costs, or a loss may be incurred.
9. Financial statements in a Management by Exception System should reflect:
   a. The plan
   b. The actual results
   c. The exceptions

Index

INDEX